Loose Ends
and Extras

CHAMBERS'S EDUCATIONAL COURSE.

Abraham Briggs

INTRODUCTION
November 17th 1872
TO THE SCIENCES

LONDON
W. & R. CHAMBERS 47 PATERNOSTER ROW
AND HIGH STREET EDINBURGH
1872.

Loose Ends and Extras

Asa Briggs

Frontline Books
London

Loose Ends and Extras
First published in 2014 by Frontline Books,
an imprint of Pen & Sword Books Ltd,
47 Church Street, Barnsley, S. Yorkshire, S70 2AS
www.frontline-books.com

Copyright © Asa Briggs, 2014

The right of Asa Briggs to be identified as the author of this work
has been asserted by him in accordance with the
Copyright, Designs and Patents Act 1988.

ISBN: 978-1-84832-773-3

CIP data records for this title are available from the British Library

For more information on our books, please visit
www.frontline-books.com, email info@frontline-books.com
or write to us at the above address.

Printed and bound by CPI Group (UK) Ltd, Croydon, CR0 4YY

Typeset in 11.25/15 pt Minion Pro

Contents

Dedication

I dedicate this book to my friends Monique Grandjean
and Doris White, on whom my life has depended,
now depends and will depend in the future.

In loving memory of my father and grandfather.

Illustrations

Frontispiece: This revealing book of 1872 was bought in London by my grandfather, Abraham Briggs, before he became an engineering apprentice in Leeds, the city of his birth. He gave it to me when I was an undergraduate in Cambridge, just before the Second World War began. I did not know anything then about W. & R. Chambers who conducted their business in Edinburgh and Paternoster Row in London, where their office was destroyed in the Blitz.

Acknowledgements

I would like to acknowledge with gratitude the patience and fortitude of my publisher, Michael Leventhal, and of Stephen Chumbley and Donald Sommerville. I would not have been able to write the book without the support, as always, of Pat Spencer. Nor could I have found it possible to complete it without the unfailing support of the present Vice-Chancellor of Sussex, Michael Farthing. He seconded to me Kees-Jan Schilt for the last two weeks before I completed my text. I have been caringly assisted with keeping and using my copious files by Nick Milner-Gulland. Finally, but not least, I acknowledge the help of my wife Susan, never easy for her on account of her failing eyesight. Any errors that may remain are entirely my own responsibility.

Chapter 1

Why This Book?

I think in threes, as I shall demonstrate throughout this book, and when my publisher (and friend) Michael Leventhal invited me to write a third book while the University of Sussex was still celebrating its golden jubilee I immediately and gladly accepted his invitation. *Loose Ends and Extras* now completes what has become a trilogy, each volume of which has appeared since my ninetieth birthday on 7 May 2011. *Secret Days: Code-breaking in Bletchley Park* appeared in 2011 and *Special Relationships: People and Places* followed a year later. The title of the first of these volumes almost chose itself. The title of the second I spent a long time thinking about as I have done also in deciding on the title of my third, *Loose Ends and Extras*.

It is a title that demands an immediate explanation. I chose it because of my interest in broadcasting. It is the name of a radio programme first presented in 1986 by Ned Sherrin, a friend of mine, himself keenly interested in broadcasting history. He did not choose the name himself, however, and the new programme that he was presenting certainly did not appeal at the time to most radio critics. Yet in its first year it attracted a large listening audience and it went on to win a prestigious Sony Award for the Best Magazine Programme of the Year. It still runs in 2014 and is now presented by Clive Anderson. Like Ned, with whom he overlapped as presenter, Clive is involved in a large number, almost countless, of other well-known radio programmes.

Ned deserves attention at the beginning of what I call my *Loose Ends* because of his extraordinarily wide range of activities and personal contacts. He wrote two autobiographies setting out the details. He was born in the Somerset Levels, so much in the news in 2014, the son of a gentleman farmer, and after two years of military service with the Royal Corps of Signals, beginning as I did at its headquarters in Catterick, he entered Exeter College, Oxford, which again figures in quite different contexts in this *Loose Ends*. He was studying law and actually became a barrister, but devoted much of the time to taking part in plays and reviews. He became involved in television in 1956, the first full year of commercial television programmes, first employed not by the BBC but by Associated Television. That was because a friend from Oxford told him about it.

In 1957 Ned switched to the BBC as a temporary production assistant, working on *Tonight*, where I had many friends among its presenters, including Cliff Michelmore, Geoffrey Johnson-Smith and Alan Whicker. In 1962, with the support of Alasdair Milne and Donald Baverstock, both of whom figure prominently in my *History of Broadcasting in the United Kingdom*, as does Grace Wyndham Goldie, head of the Current Affairs department, Ned, who was absorbed in current affairs, was happy to join the Current Affairs department and not Entertainment – his *Loose Ends* radio programme was always to start with a high-speed news of the week report given by himself. His first task was to direct the BBC's first satirical programme *That Was The Week That Was*, known as *TW3*, which he described at the time with obvious pride as 'aware, pointed, irreverent, fundamentally serious, intelligently witty, outspoken in the proper sense of the term'.

These were his own personal qualities, but the programme attracted a huge mass audience, at its peak more than 13 million. His frontman, the young David Frost, was then largely unknown to the public, but was soon to be a celebrity on both sides of the Atlantic, as was Ned himself. Those people who found their unfamiliar kind of satire offensive – there were some BBC Governors among them – pilloried David and Ned as 'pedlars of filth and smut and destroyers of all that Britain holds dear'.

The audience success of what was a live show, for that was how David and Ned wanted it to be, owed much to its regular participants, Lance Percival, Willie Rushton and Millicent Martin, and they owed much to scriptwriters behind the scenes: Keith Waterhouse and Willis Hall wrote for every weekly number of *TW3*, and among the other regular writers were Bernard Levin, who also performed, and Gerald Kaufman, an Oxonian and future Labour MP, who introduced himself to Ned, who had an eye for talent. In the wake of *TW3* he devised and produced *Not So Much a Programme, More a Way of Life* with a nucleus of previously little-seen performers, among them John Bird, John Fortune and Eleanor Bron.

Although Ned never hid his homosexuality, as I look back I associate him most easily with three women, Millicent Martin, Eleanor Bron and, above all, Caryl Brahms, much older than the others or he was. Contrasting with him totally in appearance, she was small and wore large spectacles. Ned wrote for the stage with Caryl, persuading her at the beginning of their cooperation to present a theatrical version of one of Ned's favourite books which she had co-authored, *No Bed for Bacon*, at the Bristol Old Vic in 1959. They collaborated on many other dramas and musicals, including a musical biography of Marie Lloyd, *Sing a Rude Song*, and in complete contrast a play about Thomas Beecham. Just before Caryl Brahms died their boldly adventurous *The Mitford Girls* opened at the musical festival in Chichester in 1982 and was subsequently transferred to the Globe Theatre in London.

Theirs was a remarkably long span of creative collaboration, for the most part successful financially. Of course not all his stage collaborations were financial successes, but they all gave him pleasure. With Alistair Beaton he wrote two Gilbert and Sullivan up-dates, and in 1992 he directed on the London stage *The National Health* by Peter Nichols with a cast which included Jim Dale and Eleanor Bron. He also directed Keith Waterhouse's *Mr. and Mrs. Nobody*, starring Judi Dench and Michael Williams, and *Jeffrey Bernard is Unwell*, starring Peter O'Toole. He used to go with Beaton and the actors he liked to his favourite Soho pub, the Coach and Horses. Everyone believed that his knowledge of theatre lore and theatre folk was unique. Some pronounced it 'legendary'.

Off stage and screen, Ned wrote a gossip column for a theatre magazine and a restaurant column for the *Evening Standard*. He was drama correspondent for *The Oldie* and he also edited Caryl Brahms's memoirs *Too Dirty for the Windmill* (1986). During the last years of the 1960s he produced ten films, including *Up Pompeii* with Frankie Howerd. I found Howerd funny and got to know him quite well and to like him when I was writing my history of broadcasting, which Ned also enjoyed. It does not have many jokes or, indeed, anecdotes in it, but Ned never treated it simply as a work of reference.

Ned established a reputation as a raconteur and won the Benedictine 'After Dinner Speaker of the Year' competition in 1991. What better sponsor than Benedictine for a *bon viveur* who enjoyed two strong dry martinis before he went to the theatre to see a show? It was a cruel trick of fate that in the last years of his life he suffered from a throat cancer which eventually deprived him of his voice. In an obituary – and when Ned read newspapers he always read obituaries first – Alistair Beaton wrote that he wished that Ned had had the good sense to live until he was at least a hundred.

To the title of my *Loose Ends*, in which longevity is much discussed, I added the words *And Extras*, because I have set out in writing it not just to tie up loose ends in my own previous books or because I liked the word extras, which I do, but to incorporate completely new material. Not the least interesting part of this concerns the first years in the development of the sciences at the University of Sussex. I gave a well-attended jubilee lecture in the University on the subject which I have considerably extended and thoroughly revised in *Loose Ends and Extras*. In it I recall my own experiences in learning science at school, the long-standing interest of my family in practical science, and my meeting after the war many distinguished scientists across the Atlantic, including Murray Gell-Mann. He was one of the most encyclopaedic of all the great scientists I have known. His first wife, Margaret, whom I liked very much and who sadly died in 1981, was a historian from England.

The Gell-Manns lived in a charming Victorian house in Aspen, Colorado, a town which has figured much in my own life and where, from 1972, Murray was Chairman of the Board of the Aspen Institute of Theoretical Physics, founded in 1961, the year I moved to Sussex University. The Gell-Manns spent their summers in Aspen where he taught me less about theoretical physics – and he was a Nobel Prize winner in Physics in 1969 – than how to identify edible fungi with the help of plaster models of them. We went mushrooming in the Colorado mountains leading up to Independence Pass.

When we were in Aspen we also met the remarkable and indomitable Mortimer Adler, who with Robert Hutchins had organised 'Great Books' seminars at the University of Chicago. My wife attended one of his Aspen seminars. Mortimer, who as a philosopher disdained history, also married a historian. He was the great attraction in the first years of the Aspen Institute and people came to his seminars from all walks of life. Many were businessmen.

I spent my first post-war spell in the United States in 1947, travelling across the continent. Later I worked as a Member of the Institute for Advanced Studies at Princeton University in 1953 and 1954 when Robert Oppenheimer was Director. I had my own office there. An aged and white-haired Albert Einstein was also established in the Institute, and each day I would travel with him in a large Institute car from the middle of the town of Princeton to the Institute building. It was not from either man, however, that I learned any physics. There were young theoretical physicists at the Institute, my own contemporaries, from whom I learned much more. I used to question them about what they were doing in physics. Then and later in my life I learned more physics from conversations with physicists than from reading books.

In what now seems a parallel chapter to my chapter on the beginnings of science at Sussex University, I use my memory and my collection of press cuttings to recall and reassess John Reith, first Director-General of the BBC, whom I knew extremely well, better than anyone I met at Princeton. He had been sent from Glasgow as a boy to a boarding school in England, Gresham's near Holt in Norfolk. He was as lonely at school in England as he was when at home in Scotland. Although I knew Reith so well, never in our relationship did I ever call him John. Nor did he ever call me Asa. Reith spent only two years at Gresham's and went back to the Glasgow Royal Technical College, now the University of Strathclyde, to study engineering and to become an apprentice at the Hyde Park Locomotive Works in Springburn.

I was impressed by the University of Strathclyde, where I knew well its Principal and Vice-Chancellor, Sam Curran, who had been appointed Principal of the Glasgow Royal College of Technology in 1959 before it became the University of Strathclyde. I liked to talk to him about science policy, for he was deeply involved in decision-making on major national issues. He was nine years older than me and I learned much from him. I was glad when his College became a University and when three of my own graduate students from Leeds and Sussex took up academic posts there. He was deservedly knighted in 1970.

I shall never forget the ceremony when Strathclyde installed its first Chancellor, Lord Todd, a most distinguished and influential chemist formerly the Master of Christ's, Cambridge. A tall god-like man, he was wearing magnificent blue robes. There was one absurd incident at his installation. The Rector of St Andrews was booed by some of the people present when he made a speech more or less suggesting that Strathclyde should never have been a university at all. St Andrews, which has a long history, never honoured me, but I was glad to be given an honorary doctorate by Strathclyde in 1973.

In recalling Reith before reassessing him I can never leave history out, and I have to go back in time to before he was a not very clever student at Glasgow Technical College. Railways and canals figured in the early life of the man who was to become first General Manager of the BBC. Curiously religion entered the Reith family history through transport. An earlier Reith, George, had been general manager of the Clyde Navigation Trust, and it was he who shaped John Reith's destiny when he persuaded John's father to enter the Presbyterian ministry. John, a complex character with many strands in his history, was a son of the manse.

In all my chapters I consider the role of memory and its inaccuracies in history. Reith distorted his memories of his own father and was not himself historian enough to grasp how judgements of one's self and of others change in the light of changing circumstances, personal and cultural. I consider in *Loose Ends and Extras* how my own memories have turned me into the historian that I am. Having moved from political and economic history to social history and through social history into cultural history, I see history as a continuum. The last chapter of my book is called 'Pasts, Present, Futures', with the fleeting present, which so quickly becomes the past, being the only one of these three to be kept in the singular. This is the most basic of all the threesomes that I write about, and the last chapter of this book concentrates on it. It is a threesome that relates to time, and in all three books which I have written since I was ninety time is at the core of my thinking and feeling.

I had been preoccupied with the study of time for years even before a brief spell in 1942 and 1943 when I was teaching history at Keighley Boys' Grammar School, and despite Piaget, who felt that school-children should not be introduced to time so soon, introduced it to my first-year pupils before turning via prehistory to ancient pre-Greek and Roman cultures. With the history went geography as it always does for me. I find it difficult to separate them. I told my young pupils of the Nile, the Ganges and the Tigris before moving on to the Thames, the Severn, the Rhine and the Rhône.

In introducing them to pre-history I introduced them to fossils also, which as a schoolboy I had collected to keep in a glass case with other objects in what I called my museum. As I reached measuring, numbering, calendars and inscriptions in my lessons at KBGS I could not neglect, and I never have neglected, chronology. I believe it to be fundamental for all students of history. Before I start writing any historical book I prepare a list of dates in chronological order and at the end of my one-volume jubilee history of the BBC, published in 1972, I appended such a list. I have referred back to it many times in writing *Loose Ends and Extras*. I had been deeply impressed when at KBGS as a boy I examined the list at the end of G. M. Young's *Portrait of an Age* which I had the prescience to choose as a school prize. Young has been a historian to whom I owe a great deal. I never agreed with his politics, but I was drawn to what he had to say about culture. He was drawn to me in turn when he read *Victorian People*, which I published in 1954. One day there was a tap on my Worcester College door and a not very academic-looking Young poked his head round the door. He told me that since I praised the art of conversation in an essay which I had written he would like to have a conversation with me.

The book which influenced me most as a historian after the end of the Second World War was Marc Bloch's *The Historian's Craft* which appeared in English in 1954. Its subtitle is *Reflections on the Nature and Uses of History and the Techniques and Methods of Historical Writing*. Bloch, born in 1886, began his book in 1941 in vanquished France and he had not completed it when, in 1944, leading a local resistance group in Lyons, he was captured by the Germans, tortured and eventually executed. He continued writing his book for as long as he could. I could never have had a conversation with Bloch.

For him the 'initial purpose of history' was the 'study of men in time', not the study of 'the past'. 'Understanding', he affirmed, is 'the beacon light of our study'. 'Misunderstanding of the present', he believed, 'is the inevitable consequence of ignorance of the past.' Yet, a climactic affirmation, it is 'the faculty of understanding the living' that is 'the master quality of the historian'.

As a brilliant medieval historian who had written learnedly of the healing powers attributed to kings, Bloch enjoyed telling an anecdote about a trip which he had made with a greatly respected Belgian historian, Henri Pirenne, to Stockholm early in the 1930s. They had scarcely arrived there when Pirenne asked Bloch what they should go to see first, adding that 'it seems there is a new city hall here. Let's start there.' Warding off Bloch's possible surprise, Pirenne went on 'If I were an antiquarian I would have eyes only for the old stuff, but I am a historian. Therefore I love life.'

In my own reflections on time I never approach history as an antiquarian, although I am interested in the history of antiquarianism and in the Society of Antiquaries which occupies a building next to the Royal Academy. I treasure the contribution antiquarians have made to history as I do the contribution of anthropologists. When the Society of Antiquaries celebrated its tercentenary in 2007 a memorable exhibition was staged in the Royal Academy which revealed how the country's material objects came to be recovered, collected, recorded and preserved. It also examined the impact of archaeology on their discovery and care.

In my own recent reflections on time I draw on mathematics, including statistics, literature, mainly English and French, art from all cultures, and music. I was a friend of the American Professor George Ford who, as President of the International Society for the Study of Time, organised in 1982 a fascinating landmark conference in Italy on 'Scientific Concepts of Time in Humanistic and Social Perspective'. One of the participants was the novelist John Fowles, author of one of my favourite books, *The French Lieutenant's Woman*, subsequently turned into a film. Another participant was the Professor of Music at Indiana University.

Music was never an extra in what I wrote about time. I read with pleasure Anthony Powell's volumes *A Dance to the Music of Time*, some of which I discussed with him, both the characters in the novels and their relationships with each other. Einstein played the violin and once told an interviewer 'If I were not a physicist I would probably be a musician. I live my daydreams in music . . . I get most of my joy in life out of music.' I myself like to meditate on the music of the spheres, and closer to home I have written about Mahler, and when and how the BBC broadcast his music, then very little heard in Britain. It is the only time that I have ever written a review in a musical journal. I was a friend of Benjamin Britten, who received his peerage on the same day as I did. We were on a very short list of names. I opened the new library building at Aldeburgh. I persuaded the University of Sussex to give an honorary degree to Peter Pears. I knew that Ben, like me, had enough honorary degrees already.

Ben had been the first recipient of the Aspen Institute's Award for the Humanities in 1964, and when, ten years earlier, the Aspen Music

Festival separated itself off from the Institute this became a very important date in my life. Ten years later I used to go to concerts in a large tent set in the meadows where I heard a wider range of music than I could hear in Britain. It was played by superb performers and an excellent programme was produced for every performance. I have kept a set and can trace my own musical progress from them. The concert I remember most is a performance of Bach's St Matthew Passion. The person sitting next to me was taken ill and died in the tent. The music festival now has a new hall provided by a benefactor friend of mine, Irving Harris, as remarkable a benefactor as the founder of the Institute, also from Chicago, Walter Paecke, who sadly died of cancer in 1960.

The Institute went on to honour many musicians and historians. There is one English historian who collected many honorary degrees and I must introduce him at this point, H. A. L. Fisher, a very different kind of historian from Marc Bloch and Pirenne in that he was totally uninterested in antiquities. I remember being antagonised by his best-selling *History of Europe* published in 1935, which I read when I was an undergraduate in Cambridge before the Second World War. I must add that Fisher was an ex-politician who had been a member of a Liberal Cabinet. He could discern no patterns in history at all and stuck to narrative. Myself I always thought of history not just as narrative but as patterns both in time and space. I chose the title *Patterns of Peacemaking* for my first book, which I co-authored with the History Fellow of Sidney Sussex, David Thomson, later the College's Master.

It is certainly not easy to discern patterns in Fisher's own life. He was born in London, but was more associated with Sheffield and, of course, Oxford. As MP for Hallam, a seat now held by Nick Clegg, he joined Lloyd George's Cabinet as President of the Board of Education and in that capacity was responsible for the 1918 National Education Act, which made school attendance compulsory for all children up to the age of fourteen. Between 1913 and 1917 he was Vice-Chancellor of the University of Sheffield and in 1918 he became MP for the Combined English Universities, a seat that no longer exists.

In 1926 he quit politics and became Warden of New College, Oxford, his own old college, after having arrived there from Winchester. In 1929 he was awarded the James Tait Black Memorial Prize for his biography *James, Viscount Bryce, OM*. An Ulster Scot born in Belfast, Bryce went to the University of Glasgow in 1854 and three years later won a scholarship to Trinity College, Oxford. In 1870 he became Regius Professor of Civil Law in Oxford, a post which he held until 1893. He wrote history books rather than legal textbooks and with Lord Acton was one of the founders of the *English Historical Review* in 1885. In the same year he became Liberal MP for South Aberdeen, having been MP for Tower Hamlets for five years.

Interested in foreign affairs and holding various posts, the most important of which was that of Ambassador to the United States, Bryce has always fascinated me. He was an early recipient of the Order of Merit. In the year that Fisher published his biography he himself received an OM. Fisher remained Warden of New College until his death in 1940. He had been knocked down by a lorry on his way in the blackout to preside over a Conscientious Objectors' tribunal.

There was a curious sequel to the story. In 1943 his high-quality woollen underpants, which were left behind in New College with his books and some of his clothes, were used in a secret intelligence coup, Operation Mincemeat, planned meticulously to deceive the Germans. A body dropped in the sea off Spain was made to appear that of a Royal Marines Officer and was wearing Fisher's underpants. It is good to know that the operation was successful. I am afraid that I was not able to discuss this with Fisher's only child, Mary Bennett, who was head of St Hilda's College. All this patternless biographical information is so fascinating that I renounce the youthful antagonism to Fisher that I felt when I read his *History of Europe*.

When I was appointed to my Fellowship at Worcester, the Warden of New College was Alix Smith, appointed in 1941, whom I liked. He was a modest man, unlike several Wardens, and used to invite me to lunch and sometimes dinner. I remember talking not about national or university politics but about haunted houses and psychic research. He was still in office when I left Oxford for Leeds, and through him

I got to know the daughters of one of the most famous of all New College Wardens, William Spooner, Warden from 1903 to 1924. Spooner gave his name to an ism, linguistic not philosophical. His daughters, who lived in North Oxford, did not attempt to copy Spoonerisms. They were renowned equally for their cycling and for their sober hospitality. They were very kind to me.

When I returned to Worcester as Provost in 1976 the Warden of New College was Sir William Hayter, whom I knew quite well as Ambassador to the Soviet Union, and through his sister, who was head of the British Council in Brussels and wrote a fascinating book on drugs in early nineteenth-century Britain. I lectured for the Council there and in other Belgian cities where I made links with many future Belgian friends. Hayter had a bigger influence, however, on my younger son's life than on mine. He persuaded me to send my younger son, Matthew, to a state school in Thame, Lord Williams's, which had a small boarding house where he got to know well as a friend a half-Norwegian boy called Cato Stonex, who has done very well in the City and whom he still sees. They recently went together with other friends on a trip to the Galapagos Islands.

Hayter's suggestion that Matthew should go to Lord Williams's has had long-term outcomes and widespread ramifications. By not going to a public school his outlook on life became independent and very much his own. Lord Williams's was a school with a very strong musical tradition. His first headmaster at Lord Williams's, Geoffrey Goodall, who soon after Matthew arrived moved to Exeter School, was the father of Howard Goodall, the composer and frequent broadcaster. The tradition continues in my own home in Lewes, for I often hear Howard Goodall.

Going back to New College another Warden who became a close friend of mine was the lawyer Harvey McGregor, a good pianist and singer, who put on musical concerts in his college which my wife Susan and I loved to attend. His helper, Pippa, was a wonderful hostess who made the very most of Harvey's garden. After Susan and I moved to Scotland Harvey followed us there to an Edinburgh house ideal for entertaining. Pippa later moved to Ireland.

Time can tick slowly and can rush by. It flows like a river with swamps and rapids, waterfalls and broad estuaries. Once we used sundials to help us measure time. Then we used clocks and watches. Gold watches were handed out as favourite retirement presents to be worn in waistcoat pockets. Wrist-watches have survived waistcoats. Did Sherrin or Frost or Oppenheimer or Einstein like watches or clocks? I write these words in our Lewes home as what we call British Summertime has come to an end. It will be lighter in the morning, darker in the afternoon. I wish that was not so, not only because I never liked having to change the clocks in my Lewes home, which I now have to get someone else to do. I treasure these clocks, particularly a grandfather clock which belonged to my parents and their parents before them. I remember my grandfather and father taking handsome gold watches out of their waistcoat pockets.

I like to think of all the wrist-watches I have worn, very few of which have survived, and most of all to recall institutional clocks which take me back through time. I can remember a plain one, rather like a railway station clock, in the first infants school, Eastwood, which I attended at the age of five. The clock on the tower of the Gothic building which housed Keighley Boys' Grammar School, which I attended from 1931 to 1938, was called locally the Mechanics Clock. Its chimes could be heard all over the town. I heard them on my way to school long before I listened to Bow Bells, which were said to have welcomed Dick Whittington to London. I have subsequently been taken to the top of the tower of Big Ben to listen to the chimes as the clock is actually chiming them. It was a great experience. The BBC made Big Ben a national, even an international, symbol as Frenchmen had made the Eiffel Tower in Paris such a symbol and Americans the Statue of Liberty as you travelled by water to New York's dockland.

Railway clocks, like that at Victoria, have to be visible from a distance if you are not to miss a train. Railway timetables I have depended upon in all my travels, as I appreciated long before I watched Michael Portillo on television travelling in Britain and in Europe with a copy of Bradshaw in his hand. I think he is right to make much of Bradshaw, but I would like to have seen continental Europe through Baedeker's eyes as well as Bradshaw's. I used to love to search for copies of Baedekers that I did not own on bookstalls by the Seine in Paris. Some booksellers specialised in them.

When we turn to Bradshaw's British and Irish guides we realise how many railways we have lost since the Beeching report. I liked Beeching as a person, and I do not think he should be demonised as he often has been since his report came out. Some losses of railways were necessary. Nevertheless, I consider that the old Great Central should have been kept with its links between Bradford and Marylebone and I wish that when many local lines were closed the rails should not have been torn up. I salute the volunteers who have brought several closed lines into use again. One of them is the Bluebell Line not far from Lewes. I would also like the ravaged line from Lewes to Uckfield opened up to passengers again. In the seventh chapter of *Loose Ends and Extras*, 'Words, Links, Coincidences' it is the connecting word in the threesome title.

In my 'Abiding Historical Interests', another threesome, my title for Chapter 5, I start not with trains but with shops which do not usually have clocks outside them. The history of retailing is one of the three branches of history that I have actively cultivated, along with the history of sport and the history of health. They have links with each other and all bring in time as a dimension. Shops change, games change, bathrooms change.

When in the 1980s I was preparing my well-illustrated centennial history of the great retailers Marks and Spencer, I used to tell the time from a pendulum clock in the boardroom in Michael House, then the company's business headquarters, in Baker Street, not far from where Sherlock Holmes is said to have lived. Presented to the board by a manufacturing firm that depended for its success on M&S taking the goods that it produced to sell in its stores throughout the country, the clock carried on it a verbal message, 'Time marches on'.

This, probably by coincidence, was the slogan used across the Atlantic by Henry Luce, from his office in the 48-storey Time Life building in the Rockefeller Center in the heart of Manhattan. Luce was the publisher of *Life*, a pictorial 'window on the world', which no longer survives in the age of television, *Fortune*, famous for picking out its 'Fortune 500', the biggest companies in the world, and *Sports Illustrated*, a weekly read not only by sports fans but by sports players. The fourth of his pioneering companies, *Time Magazine*, with a worldwide readership, survives. It makes history as well as records it. During its long life it has had significant and controversial changes in ownership, some involving bitter struggles between individuals and interests, but throughout and after all of them I have continued to subscribe to *Time* and regularly to read it. I keep a list of all its 'men of the year' and was delighted that Pope Francis was chosen as its Man of 2013.

There is a multitude of threesome slogans concerned with time, among them 'savour the moment', 'it's about time', 'just in time', 'time to unwind', 'not just yet', and perhaps the once most familiar of all in England 'time gentlemen please'. There are also threesome sets of initials abbreviating the names of institutions, three of which stand out in 'the inside story' of *Loose Ends and Extras*, BBC, MCC and UGC. The use of such acronyms offends many writers on the English language. The first, BBC, refers to the institution originally in charge of British broadcasting. The BBC was set up in 1922, first as a company, then in 1927 as a corporation. When its organisation and status were so changed it did not need to change its notepaper. I explain how and why in Chapter 4, 'John Reith, Recalled, Reassessed'.

The second, MCC, refers to cricket, both a ground in Marylebone with a famous and now well-equipped members' stand, and a cricketing authority. The ground now also has a modern-looking media centre, rather more than a grandstand, offering BBC cricket pundits a perfect full-length view of the match on which they are commentating. They sometimes forget the match that they are watching and deploy history and statistics to put what they say into perspective.

The third acronym, UGC, the University Grants Committee, alas now long dead, was the public authority which, for a large part of my lifetime, received all moneys for universities' current and capital expenditures, that it had bargained for with government. The bargaining concerned not one year's requirements and provisions but five years'. The quinquennial system gave both individual universities and the UGC itself the power to plan. I regard that system as being something that we should never have lost, but I understand why it had to go, like some of the lines closed by Beeching.

I would add two other sets of threesome initials in chronicling my own post-war experiences, WEA, Workers Educational Association, of which I become Deputy President in 1954 and in succession (apostolic I thought) to R. H. Tawney, President from 1958 to 1967. There were some WEA members who would have substituted the word adult for workers in the name of their association. I believed and still believe when I am not involved in any way with the WEA that such a substitution would have been a change for the worse. The WEA, founded by Albert Mansbridge, has been in existence since 1903.

My second in this set of threesome initials I had never heard before 1945. I only heard of them when I moved from being a Cambridge undergraduate to being a Fellow and Tutor of an Oxford college. Thereafter the threesome PPE mattered in relation to my own work. I had to know its history as I had come to know the history of the WEA. PPE had been created in 1921, the year when I was born. The initials stood for philosophy, politics and economics.

In 1945 I tutored in the last two of them, unusual in Oxford, and I regret that now in 2014 undergraduates study only two out of the three. To me as a resident newcomer to Oxford in 1945 the initials PPE sounded less pompous than the two words Modern Greats, the other name given to the combination. This took its name from Greats, not pompous within its own context. Originally it was conceived of as Literae Humaniores and consisted of classical (Greek and Latin) languages, ancient history and philosophy.

Curiously the philosophy taught to Greats undergraduates was not ancient. It was the same as that studied by undergraduates reading PPE. In my own college, undergraduates reading both Greats and PPE were given tutorials by the same philosophy tutor, my colleague and friend David Mitchell. He had read Greats himself and had his rooms in Worcester on the same staircase as I did, and we both took pupils from other colleges to augment our meagre college income. I recall more than one occasion when one of his pupils from another college, Barbara, his future wife, came out of his room utterly exhausted after a Greats tutorial and would come into the quiet of my own room and chat with me to regain her balance.

The then aged Provost of Worcester, F. J. Lys, who was Provost when I first became a Fellow and Tutor, was so set in his ways that he despised philosophers who had not studied Literae Humaniores. Fortunately philosophy never complicated my own relationship with him. He liked me more for just being young rather than because I was tutoring in economics and politics.

In 1952 I published an article 'Cerberus and the Sphinx' in *Twentieth Century*, a magazine then at the peak of its own influence. It was based on a paper which I read to Balliol College undergraduates at the other end of Beaumont Street from Worcester with the Randolph Hotel on the way from one college to the other. In my paper I explained why philosophy, politics and economics made up an interesting and effective combination of three inter-related subjects. Why did I give my paper its captivating title 'Cerberus and the Sphinx'? They were strange children of strange parents. Cerberus at first had many heads, but in the period of his greatest influence he had only three. As for the Sphinx he came from neither Greece nor Rome but from Egypt, and it is he who guards the future.

My essay was reprinted in *Serious Pursuits*, the third volume in a collection of my essays which I published years later with the Harvester Press, founded by John Spiers, a pupil of mine at Sussex University and a man of great enterprise. Before he published the first of my three volumes he was not contemplating a trilogy. Indeed, he wrote in 1985 that there would be four volumes of my essays. Nor were my publishers in 1954 anticipating a trilogy when they published *Victorian People*.

My publishers were Odhams, a business which I had not previously heard of, which was recommended to me by the well-known All Souls historian A. L. Rowse. One day when I was coming out of Exeter

College in the Turl, where one of my friends, Herbert Nicholas was Fellow and Tutor in Politics, Rowse saw me, got off his bicycle and urged me passionately to 'do for Queen Victoria what I have done for Queen Elizabeth I'. I should then take what I wrote to his publisher in London, Odhams. I had no intention of doing anything for Queen Victoria, but I followed his guidance about Odhams.

At the unpretentious Odhams office in London's Long Acre I dealt with John Canning, whom I regard as my first publisher: he became a friend as well as a publisher as Michael Leventhal now is. I used to enjoy travelling to London to see him. He edited books as well as published them, some for publishers other than Odhams. He also liked to commission pieces from professional and non-professional historians. I approved of this and when I moved to Sussex University I quite deliberately appointed people to the faculty who had no academic experience. Despite my doing this the distinction between professional and non-professional historians has widened since 1954.

Although after 1954 I could without difficulty have found a more prestigious publisher for *Victorian Cities*, which I published in 1963, I remained loyal to Odhams so long as they published books, and to John. I was strongly in favour when I arrived in Sussex of appointing some members of faculty who had no previous university experience. For example I appointed Norman McKenzie, deputy editor of the *New Statesman*, whom I had met in Australia, John Roselli, prominent anti-Fascist in the days of Mussolini, and Helmut Pappé, whom I met in New Zealand, who was farming there. Unlike the other two, Pappé had been a professor at a German university before 1939, when he was forced to flee.

Victorian Cities was the best received and most widely reviewed in what by then was obviously a trilogy, and inspired many books on English cities, each with its own history, and opened up provincial history as a legitimate field of study. Curiously A. L. Rowse, who recommended Odhams to me as publisher, is best-known today not because he did 'something for Elizabeth I' but because of his wonderful book *A Cornish Childhood* (1942) and later in life *A Cornishman at Oxford* (1965) and three other books on Cornwall, not a trilogy but written in three successive years, *Cornish Stories* (1967), *A Cornish Anthology* (1968) and *The Cornish in America* (1969).

I had always been keen to call myself a provincial as opposed to being a Londoner, and when I was to write my social history I based much of my work on local history and used local sources. I thought that national history had to be based on these. Nonetheless, I was pleased to have a good review of my book in a Huddersfield newspaper, particularly since Huddersfield was not incorporated as a borough until 1865. In one of three references to it in *Victorian Cities* I described it as having its own culture and traditions, and its culture had a very strong sporting element in it, both in soccer, with Huddersfield Town, and in rugby league. There were great names associated with the development of that culture. I never wanted to leave out personalities in the kind of history I wrote.

When I wrote *Victorian People* in 1954 I had been directly influenced by a book which was not part of a trilogy – Lytton Strachey's *Eminent Victorians*, published in 1918, a book which Odhams could never conceivably have published. Nor in 1918 would Strachey conceivably have offered it to them. In a fascinating preface he began with the unforgettable statement that:

> The history of the Victorian Age will never be written: we know too much about it. For ignorance is the first requisite of the historian – ignorance which simplifies and clarifies, which selects and omits, with a placid perfection unattainable by the highest art. Concerning the Age which has just passed our fathers and our grandfathers have poured forth and accumulated so vast a quantity of information that the industry of a Ranke would be submerged by it and the perspicacity of a Gibbon would quail before it.
>
> {It is not by the] direct method of a scrupulous narration that the explorer of the past can hope to depict that singular epoch. If he is wise, he will adopt a subtler strategy. He will attack his subject in unexpected places.

In *Victorian People*, which I subtitled *A Reassessment of Persons and Themes, 1851–67*, I had adopted that subtler strategy while totally rejecting Strachey's claim that ignorance is the first requisite of the historian and his suggestion that the history of the Victorian age will never be written. Strachey wrote about only four characters, I wrote about nine. All of mine came only from mid-Victorian England. His characters sprawled across the whole century. He had no sense that it would be helpful to divide the long reign of Queen Victoria, like Gaul, into three parts.

I preceded *Victorian People* with a quotation. I love to quote. It was from a Victorian historian, J. A. Froude, writing in 1864 towards the end of what I call the mid-Victorian years.

> From the England of Miss Austen to the England of Railways and free-trade [Strachey mentioned neither] how vast the change; yet perhaps Sir Charles Grandison would not seem so strange to us now as one of ourselves would seem to our great-grandchildren. The world moves faster and faster; and the difference will probably be considerably greater. The temper of each new generation is a continual surprise.

There is much about generations in the next chapter of *Loose Ends and Extras* which I have called Nineties, Sixties, Thirties, in that order. As for surprise, I confess that I was somewhat surprised when *Victorian People* was published in the USA by the Chicago University Press one year after it was published by Odhams in London. The Chicago Press was far more prestigious than Odhams.

I knew one person in it, Alex Morin, who had been born in Tsarist Russia and loved to take me round Chicago's Russian street markets. I loved that too. He had never visited London. Later in life I got to know Maurice Philippson, chairman of the Press, which continued to publish *Victorian People* in several editions. They looked different but the content was very much the same. The Press showed no interest in *Victorian Cities* or *Victorian Things*. *Victorian Cities* had a different American publisher, Harper and Row of New York, where it came out with changes in 1970.

In the briefest of prefaces I wrote that there were many revisions and additions but that I had not changed either its shape or its main lines of argument. Since 1963 there had been a 'boom' both in Victorian studies and in urban studies. I ended this short preface with a sentence that it was 'a companion to *Victorian People* and I was planning to complete a trilogy with a book called *Victorian Things*'. When in 1996 the Folio Society produced a beautifully illustrated version of what was now generally regarded as the Victorian trilogy, I did change significantly the content of the three volumes.

Sadly when I completed my own Victorian trilogy with *Victorian Things* in 1988 Odhams were not publishing history books, and so, never having employed a literary agent, I sent my text direct to Brian Batsford, the third of my publishers to become a friend. I had already published with him in 1956 *Friends of the People*, a study of Britain's first provincial department store, created in 1856 by David Lewis of Liverpool, who had started his business life with a small retail firm of tailors and outfitters learning business methods the hard way. He was to change business methods drastically as he created his huge store, the first of a provincial cluster. Lewis was a dazzling showman who subsequently opened a chain of department stores, including in Manchester, Birmingham, Leeds, Hanley, Leicester and Bristol. I will write fully about Lewis and those who followed him when I deal in Chapter 5 with retailing as the first of my 'Abiding Historical Interests'.

In a foreword to *Friends of the People* the Earl of Woolton noted that the enemy bombs that destroyed so much of Liverpool also destroyed most of the records which would have shown the material history of Lewis's. It was not just for that reason, however, that I included so many illustrations in my history. They were as essential in making a good book on retailing as they were to be to me when I was working on *Victorian Things*, a more pioneering book than any other that I have written. I could feel when I looked at goods in a retail shop or needle factory that I was examining primary sources as relevant to me as when I was reading documents in an archive.

Advertisements in pictures as well as in words have figured prominently in much of my writings and I was honoured to be invited to give a lecture on advertising to the Advertising Standards Authority which, when it abbreviates its name into initials, is copying my name. Batsford, my publishers, were happy that I included as many illustrations in my history. I was not primarily thinking about such publishing contents and publishing arrangements when I chose to add *And Extras* to *Loose Ends* in the title of this book.

I chose the word *Extras* primarily because I like the word extras in itself and for itself. It has multiple meanings and points in at least three directions – to sport, to food and to film. In cricket it refers to runs not made by the bat, and in soccer to time added on to a match because of injuries and interruptions after the basic ninety minutes are over. In food it refers to items on a menu for which an additional charge is made if you choose them. In film it refers to actors not individually named, usually those taking part in crowd scenes. As I complete this book, still learning a lot about extras, I see in the *Sun* a page called 'Beauty EXTRA' and on radio hear of the debut of a new music station to compete with Radio 2, Capital Extra.

Going back in time to the University of Sussex, in the year when I became Vice-Chancellor I met Richard Attenborough, who was filming *Oh! What a Lovely War*, a film about the Great War. I have devoted a whole chapter of *Loose Ends and Extras* to the First World War, Chapter 6, 'Why Remember It?' *Loose Ends and Extras* will be published in the centenary year of the beginning of the Great War. Dickie, as I very soon called him – everybody did – knew Brighton long before I did when he took the lead part in the dark and powerful film *Brighton Rock*, made in 1947 and centring on Brighton Races. He had joined the RAF Film Unit in 1943, by a coincidence the same year when I arrived as a code-breaker in Bletchley Park. Now, a quarter of a century on, he asked me whether I would allow him to invite Sussex University students to take part in *Oh! What a Lovely War* as extras. I replied immediately in two words, 'of course'.

Within a few weeks of my writing 'of course' I saw some Sussex students dressed in First World War uniforms as I crossed from the ticket office in Victoria Station to the Lewes/Eastbourne platform where I got my train home. Outside the station I felt I heard news vendors yelling out 'Extra'. There was a plethora of 'real news' in 1968 and I felt that I must be up-to-date in knowing what was happening. There was then no round-the-clock news on radio or television. Its advent ushered in a new era in media history. Newspapers were never to be the same as they had been. And there were no free newspapers to be handed out at stations in 1968.

Neither Dickie nor I could possibly have foreseen in 1968 that thirty years later he would become a very distinguished Chancellor of Sussex University. Already by then he had done much for the University as Pro-Chancellor from 1970 to 1998, and he had produced and directed in 1980 the greatest of his films, *Gandhi*, which had taken him to South Africa as well as India. Subsequently he had become President of a newly created Gandhi Foundation.

Dickie was created a baron in 1993, his seventieth birthday year, and my wife and I returned to the University for a marvellous party that he gave to celebrate it, where we met many other guests, including Bryan Forbes, actor, scriptwriter and movie mogul, whom I knew already and admired. His first success had been *The Angry Silence* (1960), made on a shoestring by Beaver Films, a company which he and Dickie had set up. It was a gripping story of a worker who refused to join a political strike and was sent to Coventry by workmates and lost an eye in a fight. Its makers were no more afraid of exposing union excesses than Graham Greene, who wrote the story of *Brighton Rock,* or John Boulting who directed that film, were afraid of exposing petty crooks, racketeers and spivs.

I did not talk to Bryan about that film at Dickie's birthday party. He died early in 2013 when I was beginning to write *Loose Ends and Extras*. I did, however, talk at the party to another guest, Ben Kingsley, about Dickie's film *Gandhi*, in which he had just starred in the title role. I found it interesting to talk to him – his surname had resonances for me – and I was delighted when he was knighted in 2002.

Long before Dickie's great party Susan and I had often travelled to Richmond to meet 'darling' Dickie and his wife Sheila in their lovely home, Old Friars. While we were there we sometimes met guests from distant parts of the world, including India and South Africa. Some of them were film stars. We also got to know their son Michael, born in 1950, who in 1972 took his degree in English at Sussex University. Tragically Dickie and Sheila lost one of their two daughters, Jane, in the tsunami of 2004.

In his birthday year Dickie produced and directed the popular film *Jurassic Park* that frightened its British and American viewers as it took them back millions of years in time. Imaginatively, and with striking special effects, it brought to the screen terrifyingly realistic-looking prehistoric animals. In the film it was the sight of real prehistoric animals that attracted eager visitors to Jurassic Park, and safely in our homes or in cinemas we watched their reactions. We saw the animals induce havoc and horror for those who managed the Park, as well as visitors who had sometimes travelled great distances and paid substantial entrance fees.

While Dickie was producing his films his brother David, slightly younger than he was, had pioneered a huge number of wildlife films showing 'real' animals, reptiles, birds, mammals and astonishing oceanic creatures. I had met David through the BBC when he was a lively Controller of BBC2: he had, for example, commissioned *Monty Python's Flying Circus*. I hoped as historian of the BBC that he would become the BBC's next Director-General and believed that he would have been an outstanding one; but he soon made it clear that he preferred travelling through the world looking at animals to commissioning programmes. Sometimes the animals were previously unknown species inhabiting hitherto unexplored tropical forests and ocean depths, in the most inaccessible places. Everywhere David went he was accompanied by a team of brilliant photographers, who combined daring and patience.

As his experience of recording nature deepened, the technology of filming was being transformed. All kinds of creatures, including plants and flowers, earthworms and insects were filmed at close hand using time-lapse cameras, often over a long period of time. It was now possible both to slow down time and to speed it up. Among the insects filmed were Sussex fireflies, which I used to watch in my friend Tim Renton's house near Lewes. I failed in my efforts to transfer some of them to my then home, Ashcombe House, a long walk across the Sussex Downs. I was interested that in his filming David from time to time returned to places he had known in his Leicestershire childhood when he was a serious collector of fossils.

For him as a wildlife specialist books usually accompanied films. His first book on his travels, *Zoo Quest to Guiana*, appeared in 1956, to be followed by five other *Zoo Quests* between then and 1961. In 2009 he published his prize-winning *Life Stories*, to be followed by *New Life Stories* two years later. Through the unique quality of his films and illustrated books David richly deserved all the honours conferred upon him, including in 2005 the greatest honour that the nation can bestow, the OM. Happily he is still on quest as I write this book. The paths followed by Dickie and David have now met, for David has given his support to a project for a Jurassic Park-style attraction in Dorset complete with animatronic dinosaurs.

It is a strange coincidence that while I am writing *Loose Ends* academics from different countries are meeting at the Royal Society in London to discuss DNA mapping. The news leads journalists to talk of a breakthrough. Giant Ice Age beasts may be 're-created'. Whether they can or cannot, the discovery of DNA gave a new dimension to the study of Darwinian evolution.

David at eighty-seven is full of energy and began his Christmas *Tweet of the Day* on Radio 4 with the sound of 'our feathered friend, the robin'. While I have been writing *Loose Ends and Extras* television cameras have devoted hours of broadcasting to British wildlife watched at close quarters in nature reserves in different parts of the country, including the metropolis, and in each of the four seasons of the year. Skilled observers trace the migration of birds and of fishes, dealing sympathetically but unsentimentally with the facts of life both of predators and victims and with their rearing of offspring.

Because of my own lack of physical mobility I watch more television than I ever used to do, and wildlife programmes specially appeal to me. I am interested too in comparing animal behaviour and human behaviour. The natural sciences and social studies meet at this point as they often do in the media. Immigration and emigration are seldom ever out of the news in 2013 and 2014. They inflame both interests and passions. Because of this, human migrations and the migrations of birds and fishes which follow a regular pattern that can be ecologically explained may not be strictly comparable.

There is, however, a pattern in human migrations too. Inside Europe, loosely controlled politically as it is, immigrants move from east (Romania and Bulgaria) to west. They also move or try to move north from the Mediterranean south and from Africa below it, on the way necessarily having to cross the Mediterranean. Often they follow circuitous routes, sometimes paying significant sums to secure passage on their would-be last stage in overcrowded boats. There were two human disasters there in the last months of 2013 which hit the news headlines. Scores of immigrants were drowned off small Italian islands. There were enquiries but no solutions.

In the United Kingdom, far from the Mediterranean, immigration policy has been divisive politically both between Conservatives supporting the coalition government in the House of Commons and Labour Party MPs in opposition. The size of the foreign-born population rose from about 3.8 million in 1993 to over 7 million in 2011, the majority of them from India and Pakistan and from Poland. Since 2010 there has been an annual cap on those from outside the European Community, but this generates continuing debate. Substantial numbers of people do not want any immigrants at all. In Switzerland, outside the European Community, there was a referendum on whether the country should curb immigration. The media in Britain hailed the result, a small majority in favour of restricting immigration, as odd given Switzerland's record in allowing people to enter it. 'One flew over the cuckoo's nest'.

There was debate too, sometimes strident, in Australia, to which immigrants from Indonesia and Malaysia travelled south, risking their lives on the oceans. Significant numbers have died. The difference between legal and illegal immigration was as important in Australia as it was in the United States. Because of geography it has been far more difficult to keep the illegals, mainly from Mexico, out of the

United States, where there is no clear-cut border, than it has been in Australia where people must arrive by sea.

Emigration of animals and of people does not figure at all in any of my collected essays, the first and second volumes of which appeared simultaneously in 1985, the first of them dealing with *Words, Numbers, Places, People*, all subjects which I still write about, the second with *Images, Problems, Standpoints, Forecasts*. By the time that a third volume of essays, *Serious Pursuits, Communications, and Education*, appeared in 1991, the year of my seventieth birthday, one of the busiest years of my long life, Harvester Press had become Harvester Wheatsheaf, a division of Simon and Schuster International Group. This division had its British headquarters not in Brighton but in Hemel Hempstead.

The last essay in *Serious Pursuits* I called 'Back to Keighley'. Ironically for me the year 1991 meant back to Brighton. Not only did I cease to be Provost of Worcester College, caught up in a round of fond farewells and champagne parties, but I had been asked to deliver the prestigious Ford Lectures in Oxford on 'Culture and Communications in Victorian England'. No one had given Ford Lectures on this topic before me.

Serious Pursuits was for me an essential supplement to the two previous volumes of what had now become a trilogy. It had not been preconceived as such. In a foreword to it, however, I wrote that the preparation of a third volume had always been part of my plan. I knew that any selection of pieces from my published work that did not include articles and lectures on communications and on education would be bound to be incomplete. I stressed that in this last volume the lectures were as significant as the articles since lectures were a major element both in communication and in education. I mentioned the Granada Lectures, organised by Granada Television, which stimulated as much interest as the Reith Lectures.

My own Granada Lecture figured in a Panther paperback called *Only Connect*, the title of a current television programme. I might have chosen that title for *Loose Ends and Extras* instead, for, as I have already shown, all things do connect, sometimes surprisingly. My lecture in *Only Connect* was called *University Challenge*, a title also taken from a television game show. The University of Sussex won it in 1968 when I was Vice-Chancellor. I have kept the empty champagne magnum which we drank in celebration. The programme then was presented by Bamber Gascoigne, a good friend. It continues with a very different presenter, Jeremy Paxman.

In *Loose Ends and Extras* I place Jeremy Paxman within a very different context, that of my Chapter 6 on 'The Great War. Why Remember It and How?' Determined that we should, he starts his four-episode TV series on the war with Big Ben counting out the seconds to the announcement of the start of the war with Germany on 4 August 1914. He laments the dead without suggesting that they died for nothing. He seems the perfect presenter. As one critic remarks, the furrows in his brow echo the trenches. This was a trench war, far longer than had been expected in August 1914. There were some people who thought it would be over by Christmas. When it did end on 11 November 1918, it was with an armistice not with a peace.

I have felt as strongly as Paxman that we should remember what happened between 1914 and 1918 and speculate on the outcome of the war. No single book has inspired what I write about the Great War in *Loose Ends and Extras*, although if I were to pick one out it would be the American Paul Fussell's *The Great War and Modern Memory*, published by the Oxford University Press in 1975. Fussell had been wounded while fighting as a lieutenant in Alsace in 1944 and had been awarded the Bronze Star and Purple Heart. He was, therefore, drawing on his personal experience of war.

My memory does not reach back to the Great War, but I have already mentioned my personal connection with the great University of Chicago, which had published *Victorian People* in 1955. I listened to lectures there before I gave a lecture there myself, and on several occasions since then I have spent a 'quarter' as a professor there. That was how the University divided its academic year, and it made it easy for me to get there from my base in England. I used to stay there at its always welcoming Faculty Club and make use of its splendid University library. I made many friends in the University, among them

Bill and Shirley Letwin and the historian Daniel Boorstin, who was then primarily interested in the relationship between law and history. He was later greatly to extend his range to encompass social and cultural history. His wife Ruth loved to share in our discussions, and I was as proud as they were when Daniel was appointed Librarian of Congress in Washington. Susan and I used to stay with the Boorstins on visits to the national capital. We were sometimes there in cherry-blossom time.

Chicago, Washington and New York are three very different cities, and all three of them have great libraries that have figured prominently in my intellectual life. I got to know the Library of Congress well in 2007 when I was made Kluge Professor. Jim Billington, Daniel's successor as Librarian of Congress, a historian of Russia and much else, whom I had met years earlier in Princeton, invited me to take up the Kluge Professorship to work on early American and British broadcasting. Paul Kluge, a businessman who had himself been involved in communications, endowed the chair.

Much of my research when I was in my eighties was on the comparative early history of broadcasting in Britain and the United States. Sharing the same communications technology, we developed quite different broadcasting systems. Why? I have written parts of a book on this subject, which is still not finished, trying to answer this question. I do not think that it was just because of Reith. With the help of Susan I have collected a mass of relevant articles and cuttings which I will go back to when *Loose Ends and Extras* is finished. While in the Library of Congress, I was working in the nearby offices of the Director of Scholarly Programs, Prosser Gifford. Among people working there at the time were Alistair Horne, a great friend whom I knew well in England (and his wife Sheelin, who was a daughter of Lord Eccles), and the Czech playwright and politician, Vaclav Havel, a really great man. While in the Library he was writing not a book but a play.

In Washington we stayed in the Cosmos Club, my favourite club in the world. On a previous visit to Washington I had been a Fellow of the Smithsonian Institute which managed a great museum full of things that fascinated me as much as books did. I planned originally that in *Loose Ends and Extras* I would include a chapter on libraries and archives, the last of the libraries the new Birmingham Library which was inaugurated since I started this book. The resources of the old library, for which I feel a certain nostalgia, were opened up to me by Valerie Norris, without whose help I could never have written my *History of Birmingham*. When then and later I went to work in New York, a city I came to love almost as much as Chicago, I spent hours working in the great New York Public Library in a section endowed by the founder of Reader's Digest, a business for which I edited several books. Like my M&S centennial history they do not figure among the books in my *Who's Who* entry. Sadly Reader's Digest has fallen on bad times. It may have been disposed of by its last owner and cease to exist. How are the mighty fallen!

I end *Loose Ends and Extras* with two short chapters, the first called 'Words, Links, Coincidences', the second another threesome 'Pasts, Present and Futures'. In my last chapter I have deliberately put the first and third of these key words for all historians not in the singular, as they are usually put, in the plural. There are alternative pasts and there are alternative futures, although there are events in the past and none in the future. I have been interested as much in futures as in pasts, although I bring the two together in a continuum. I did so years ago in an essay on forecasts in my *Collected Essays* which I called 'The Nineteenth Century Faces the Future'. I included a picture in it of *The Nineteenth Century* periodical. It later changed its name to *The Nineteenth Century and After*. It was first edited by James Knowles, an architect as well as a writer, who found a place in it for science as well as the arts and every kind of moral and religious issue. When it changed its name to *The Nineteenth Century and After* in January 1901 it showed a Janus head facing in two directions, the one back to the nineteenth century the other looking forward to the twentieth.

I observed that, at the end of the nineteenth century, newspapers and periodicals were vying with each other in producing balance sheets of gains and losses since the century began, and I gave as a characteristic example the 31 December 1899 issue of Alfred

Harmsworth's *Daily Mail*, founded as recently as 1896, two years after he and his brother Harold had acquired the *Evening News*. That 1899 issue began with the proud but now totally dated words 'The genius of a masterful race turns instinctively to forecast more readily than to retrospect, its leaders are ever more prone to prophecy than to search for precedent.' Very appositely for me given the title of this book, this issue of the *Daily Mail* was called 'Golden Extra'.

Harmsworth, 'the Chief', who liked every number of the *Daily Mail* to be full of original stories linking present to future, could not have forecast his own fate. He followed the advice of the founder of the Paris *Figaro*, whom he liked to quote: 'You must throw your pebble into the pond every day'. He launched another newspaper, the *Daily Mirror*, in 1903, in the first instance designed to appeal to women, which survived only when more space was devoted to illustrations, the size of the pages was reduced and its price was cut to a halfpenny, the original price of the *Daily Mail*. The *Daily Mirror* and the *Daily Mail* were to move in entirely different directions, the latter reaching the height of its influence during the Second World War.

In the Birthday Honours list of June 1901 Alfred Harmsworth was made a baronet, Edward VII describing him privately as 'a great power in the Press', and in 1905 he became a peer, Baron Northcliffe. He liked a conventional title, but he always put the dynastic power of his own family first. He had five brothers who held family conferences, the oldest of them, Harold, who in 1913 became Viscount Rothermere, was a financial wizard with whom Alfred cooperated as closely as he could as he rose to power. He bought primeval forests in Newfoundland to ensure that Harmsworth newspapers and periodicals were never short of paper, the product on which newsprint depended. Harold was the initiator here, Alfred was uneasy. Paper-making is a technical matter. He knew everything about newspapers and nothing about newsprint.

Harold won him over, however, and Alfred acquired a house in Grand Falls, Newfoundland, among the pulp and paper mills. His London house was very different, a townhouse in Berkeley Square, next door to that of Lord Rosebery, Liberal politician of renown, who owned a horse that won the Derby in 1897. Alfred bought the *Observer*, the oldest and most famous of English Sunday papers, in 1905 for £5,000. It proved to be a rare failure for him and he disposed of it to Lord Astor in 1913. In 1908 he acquired *The Times*. This was a success. He saved it from financial collapse. Could Alfred then have foreseen that six years later Britain and Germany would be at war? He neither hated the Germans nor desired war. Indeed, he had German relatives.

There was little music in the story of the Harmsworths, but it is in the story of Gilbert and Sullivan that I find my outstanding three-somes. Gilbert's name always came first when their Savoy operas were performed. But Richard D'Oyly Carte, born in Soho in 1844, was the man of enterprise and vision who built the theatre that gave its name to all their operas. It was the first theatre in London to be lit by electric light. I myself associate the name Savoy not with the theatre but with the hotel and with an era in BBC history.

When I look back to Gilbert, Sullivan and D'Oyly Carte, however, I enter into a world of threes. Three days after the death of Sullivan's mother he began writing the music of *Iolanthe*. On 1 May 1883 he received a letter from Gladstone to tell him that he was to receive a knighthood for his services in promoting 'the art of music'. Three musicians went to Windsor to receive it for the same reason. The other two were George Grove, the author of *Grove's Dictionary of Music and Musicians*, and the composer George Macfarren. At the Leeds Festival of 1883 – the festivals were held every three years – Sullivan conducted the new Gilbert and Sullivan opera *Princess Ida* where 'the Band', he judged, played only three wrong notes.

Three weeks after the production at the Savoy Theatre of *Princess Ida* Sullivan told D'Oyly Carte that he did not want to stage any more Gilbert and Sullivan operas at the theatre, but after the failure of a dinner *à trois* to break the deadlock Gilbert finally broke it by offering *The Mikado*, which opened in March 1885. This was an immediate success. There was a treble encore for 'Three Little Maids from School Are We'. Soon three other companies were touring the provinces while the Savoy company filled the theatre to capacity. *The Mikado* was the first Gilbert and Sullivan opera that I saw as a boy of ten in Denholme, the industrial village near Keighley where my mother was born. It had been the first Gilbert and Sullivan opera to be fully recorded in 1917.

When I was a boy at Keighley Boys' Grammar School I learnt music from a master who lived in Denholme. Not far away, Herbert Butterfield the eminent historian, who had been a boy at the same school as I, lived in another industrial village, Oxenhope, just across the moors. I occasionally went on walks with him. He relates to Chapter 3 of this book, 'Development of the Sciences at Sussex University', in which I trace my personal interest in science and the books that I read which fostered it. The relevant one by Butterfield was called *The Origins of Modern Science*.

In turning now to other younger historians who have influenced me I try to identify those, like me, who think in threes. While at school I did not learn the Latin phrase *omne trium perfectum*, 'everything that comes in threes is perfect', but looking back I do not feel that I needed it to shape my thinking. Nor, I think, did Natalie Davis. I greatly admire her writings, but sadly I have never met her. In 1995 she published a widely acclaimed study *Women on the Margin: Three Seventeenth-Century Lives* in which she compared three seventeenth-century women, one Jewish, one Catholic and one Protestant. Born in Detroit in 1929, then a thriving city, home of Henry Ford and his great automobile works, Natalie was the daughter of a rich immigrant Jewish family. As a Jewish woman brought up there she could look at Catholics and Protestants as an outsider and draw comparisons that might not have been drawn by other historians. I have no evidence, however, to suggest that her background made her think in threes or whether she feels that she does.

In 1983 she had written an engrossing best-seller, *The Return of Martin Guerre*, which focused on a trial in 1560 of a Languedoc peasant who had been missing for twelve years and had then reappeared to be accepted as the real Martin Guerre by his family and community. After a few years, however, his wife accused him of being an imposter and he appealed to the court to recognise him as the missing villager. At the very moment when the court met, the real Martin Guerre appeared. This seemed perfect material for a film, and a highly successful film was made out of it with Gérard Dépardieu playing the parts both of the genuine and the false Martin Guerre.

Through the film and its subsequent Hollywood remake Natalie became well-known outside academic circles, but she remained prominent as a historian in these circles too. Her essays and books, sometimes in translation, guaranteed her international reputation as a historian in several different countries. Being a woman writing about women, eight years before *The Return of Martin Guerre* she had published a volume of essays *Society and Culture in Early Modern France*. When she turned later in her life from single specific cultures to what she called 'cultural mixture' she made three points about the mix. First, it existed. Second, historians needed better tools to tackle it. Third, while cultural mix can have 'unfortunate features', it can have very positive ones. I agree with all three points, adding that when I think of cultural mix myself I think first of fusion food. The world's cuisine has been dramatically changed since people began to eat it.

There were also personal links that drew me to Natalie Davis's writing. She established her reputation as a historian in the great city of Lyons in France, incidentally a city of great restaurants and the city where Marc Bloch was shot in 1944. In 1948 I myself had chosen Lyons as the city outside Paris which I wanted to compare with Birmingham. Like her I was interested both in the social structure of Lyons and its social dynamics, including the incidence of violent uprisings there. More generally I was interested, as I believe she is, in the comparative history of cities. I was almost as fascinated by film as she was, and for seven years I was a Governor of the British Film Institute. I continue to receive regular information from the Institute and to read what are often very stimulating articles in *Sight and Sound*.

I learned a great deal about Natalie Davis's experiences and outlook from the highly innovative book by Maria Lúcia G. Pollares-Burke in which she recorded interviews with nine scholars, questioning them about their major and sometimes their minor works and their relation to other historians and specialists, particularly anthropologists. She

herself is a Professor of History at the University of São Paulo in Brazil
and she is married to Peter Burke, who was a key figure in the early
years of the University of Sussex. Peter was another of the nine
scholars she interviewed. So was Robert Darnton, who wrote about
the literary underground of pre-1789 France. His father was a
journalist and he himself started working life as a journalist.

I had visited Brazil several times before I met Maria Lúcia, excited
by Rio and its contrast with the new capital Brasilia, to which I was
invited by Zeff Barbu, a Romanian, who had been first Professor of
Sociology in the University of Sussex in 1973. Zeff knew of my
attachment to the great Brazilian historian Gilberto Freyre, who taught
me among other things how to integrate documentary and visual
histories. The first book of his that I read was his *The Mansions and
the Shanties*, a rich sequel to his pioneering volume *The Masters and
the Slaves*, published in 1933. Outstanding in the literature of social
history, they are works of literature in their own right, a brilliant
demonstration that anthropology, psychology and sociology can re-
create a sense of the wholeness of past life. They are big volumes and
take me beyond Bloch, though Freyre would have thoroughly
endorsed what Bloch and his friend saw, did and felt on their trip to
Stockholm. What Freyre writes about architecture and cuisine still
inspires me in 2014, a year when Brazil hosts the football World Cup.
I am distressed that my physical immobility prevents me from going
to some of the matches and to some of the cities which I have not seen
on my visits to Brazil since I first went to Rio and Brasilia.

In particular I have never visited São Paulo, and I confess that I was
cross when a symposium was held there on 'shock cities', one of the
few historical terms that I invented myself, and I was not invited to
take part in it. I had described Manchester in *Victorian Cities* as a
shock city of the 1830s and 1840s, comparing it with Los Angeles and
São Paulo in the twentieth century. One huge city in China, Wuhan,
would be on any shock city tour. I watched a television programme
largely about it presented by Robert Peston that made me want to go
there immediately. I saw it once when it was a smoky, polluted place
which made me think back to the smoky, polluted Manchester which

attracted visitors from continental Europe to look at it for themselves. Now in Mayor Tan's Wuhan I would look at it in wonder and awe.

In the first of the 'confessions and conversations with historians' which Maria Lúcia recorded, Jack Goody, British anthropologist and historian, talked much about China. Once when his assistant from Hong Kong retired, an Italian friend of his tried to stop him giving her a bunch of yellow chrysanthemums because in Italy they were flowers that you gave to the dead. 'Little did he know that in China the same flower carries a message of long life.' Goody published in 1993 a fascinating book, *The Culture of Flowers*. My next and last chapters are also concerned with longevity, but I have no chrysanthemums to adorn what I have to say. With daffodils in a vase in front of me on the table on which I am writing and a white orchid on the windowsill, I am a perfect Goody reader. Appropriately we are very near to St David's Day.

Maria Lúcia titled her book *The New History*. I confess that even in 2002 I did not consider myself to be a new historian. I am suspicious of the adjective new, first bandied about everywhere in the 1890s, particularly when it has been applied to politics, as in 'New Labour', or to communities, as in 'new towns', like Milton Keynes where the Open University has its headquarters not far from Bletchley Park. I am uneasy even about 'new universities', thoroughly debased concept that it now is. Examining in 2013 Aspen Institute's Communications and Society Program to which I regularly contributed, I find that in 2003 Aspen in Colorado staged workshops called 'New Voices, New Media Vehicles'. It claimed that they were 'revisiting the national dialogue'. I am not sure, looking back, that they were. I have also found out that in 1967 Gilberto Freyre received the Aspen Award in the Humanities.

It is not only professional historians who, I believe, think in threes. I turn back agreeably over the years to other people who have written trilogies. I think first of Philip Pullman's *The Dark Materials*, *The Subtle Knife* and *The Amber Spyglass*, a trilogy which I read in bed while spending weeks on end there in 2002 when I was suffering from deep-vein thrombosis. This has left me physically immobile ever since, confined not to bed but largely to our beautiful house in Lewes, the Caprons. We bought it in 1972 after I had become Vice-Chancellor of the University of Sussex even though we lived most of the year in the Vice-Chancellor's house, equally beautiful, Ashcombe, just outside Lewes on the road to Brighton.

The Caprons was our house for the future. It is now the context of all my work. Happily for me it is a house with a long past and with the right associations. Just outside the borough walls, it was built on waste land for Nicholas Yonge, a musician, in 1612. I do not know how much of it was built before he 'surrendered' it to the Smithiers family. Yonge died in London in 1619. In 2014 there is a flourishing Nicholas Young Music Society in Lewes putting on concerts by musicians from London and elsewhere. I am sad that because of my immobility I cannot go to hear them. The Caprons has had many families living in it since it was built and has eighteenth-, nineteenth- and twentieth-century elements in it. I find it a perfect place to write a trilogy.

Other trilogies stand out in my mind. J. R. R. Tolkien's *Lord of the Rings* which includes *The Fellowship of the Ring*, *The Two Towers* and *The Return of the Ring*, which can be compared with C. S. Lewis's 'cosmic trilogy' *Out of the Silent Planet*, *Perelandra* and *That Hideous Strength*. Both Tolkien and Lewis were older contemporaries of mine who knew each other well when I was a young newly arrived Fellow in Worcester College, Oxford. After Bletchley Park I had gone from pre-war Cambridge to post-war Oxford, Lewis had moved in the opposite direction from Oxford to Cambridge, where he found it difficult academically to fit in. English literature was a fractious subject.

F. R. Leavis of Downing College, born in 1895, edited *Scrutiny*, a kind of house journal which he had co-founded in 1932. Two years earlier he had published *Mass Civilisation, Minority Culture*, which expressed views which essentially he never changed. His followers, 'Leavisites', had distinctive views on literature in its social context. I do not know whether his wife Queenie, whose approach to literary criticism was more acceptable to me than his, ever called herself a Leavisite. At the other end of the Cambridge literary spectrum was

E. L. Tillyard, Master of Jesus College, who largely shaped the Cambridge curriculum.

David Daiches, whom I brought to Sussex in 1961, had been a Fellow and Tutor in Jesus College, when he came to be one of the first nine members of a lively new faculty. He had experience of working in many universities on both sides of the Atlantic and was in a perfect position to edit for Deutsch *Sussex: The Idea of a New University*. David, a treasured friend who went back to live in Edinburgh on retirement, wrote countless books but never, as far as I know, a trilogy.

Of the writers of the two Oxford trilogies I had fewer personal links with Lewis than with Tolkien. On retirement from Cambridge Lewis moved back to Headington in Oxford where I never even saw him. While I have been writing *Loose Ends and Extras* he has been much honoured nationally. I have heard more than one religious service devoted to him, have listened to *Screwtape Letters*, which I have never much liked, being read as 'Book of the Week', and have followed with great interest his being given a place in Poets' Corner in Westminster Abbey.

Tolkien I saw several times. He had taught English Language to Worcester College undergraduates, and in retirement lived in a large house with masses of books in La Garde-Freinet, a village in the hills above Cannes. He spent much of the year there and we had drinks with him. This was because we had friends in La Garde-Freinet, John and Ursula Sedgwick, who lived there for rather less of the year in a much smaller house. We were fond of them and their family and they come fittingly into *Loose Ends and Extras* through John's business which was carpets and Ursula's which was advertising. Ursula worked for the J. Walter Thompson Company in a very busy company house in Berkeley Square.

There I met Tom Sutton, who became the company's Managing Director in 1960 and ten years later Vice-President. He was two years younger than me, and we quickly became friends. The fact that while at the London School of Economics he became a Graham Wallas Prizeman interested me as did the fact that after leaving the LSE he did not go straight into advertising but became Research Officer of the British Marketing Research Bureau. In 1970 he won the Advertising Man of the Year Award. In all the years that I knew him we were never short of things to talk about. The fact that I knew David Ogilvy, a great advertiser, and stayed with him in his splendid house, the Château Toulou near Châtellerault in the Vienne, impressed him. I had visited Châtellerault in 1938. I remembered that knives were made there, some in retrospect devilish, all most useful and all sharp. Poitiers may even have been nearer to Ogilvy's château than Châtellerault. It is a great city where a great battle was fought between the English and the French.

With Tom Sutton I talked most about the J. Walter Thompson Company, and he encouraged me to get involved in its operations. As a result I gave lectures and chaired symposia for the company. We met in different locations, mainly in France, some of them very attractive. The first that I can remember clearly was the Château d'Artigny in the Loire department, a nineteenth-century château converted into a conference centre and hotel, the last a restaurant in the Île de France with wonderful facilities for seminars and symposia.

Before and during this last event I cooperated closely with John Treasure, a senior figure in the company who subsequently moved into what we were now beginning to call academia – which previously a few bold spirits had called 'the groves of academe'. He joined the City of London University, where many of the faculty were knowledgeable about both business and communications. I knew a great deal about the relationship between business and academia, having attended case-study discussions at the Harvard Business School and having been a Governor of the Henley Administrative Staff College from 1971 to 1979 when its Principal, Tom Kempner, reinforced my sense of the importance of drawing academics into business studies. I was naturally interested, as you will deduce from this chapter, in the Henley Centre for Forecasting. The Staff College did not restrict itself, nor did good business schools, to economics alone. As a member of the UGC I took part in discussions about the location of business schools, but I do not recall any discussions on what they should teach and how. I know that the supporters of exclusive dependence on case studies, as at the Harvard School, had a touch of the Leavisites about them.

I cannot end this chapter of *Loose Ends and Extras* without referring to two other authors of trilogies who wrote more than one of them. The first was Isaac Asimov, one year older than me, who wrote the first of his *Foundation* short stories in 1942 in the magazine *Astounding Science Fiction*. When used as an adjective not as a noun 'astounding' is more potent than the much used adjective 'incredible'. The first volume in the first of Asimov's *Foundation* trilogies, *Foundation*, appeared in 1951, *Foundation and Empire* in 1952 and *Second Foundation* in 1953. If I had not already come to love sci-fi these volumes would have converted me. They drew deep on history as they recounted the collapse and rebirth of a huge interstellar empire in a distant universe of the future.

They were so popular that Asimov wrote a second trilogy *Foundation's Edge* (1982), *Foundation and Earth* (1986) and, going back before the first trilogy, *Prelude to Foundation* (1998). He was now making much of psycho-history, which was beginning to be fashionable with some professional historians, and the role of mutants in changing the course of history. I was interested in both myself. Encouragement and good earnings drove him to write *Forward the Foundation* in 1992, the year after I left Worcester for Scotland and Lewes.

My second writer of more than one trilogy was Robertson Davies, born in Thamesville, Ontario, in 1913. His father was a newspaperman. Robertson Davies himself became editor in 1942 of the *Peterborough Examiner*, serving the 'small city' of Peterborough, north-east of Toronto, a great city (no inverted commas needed) which played an interesting part in my life fifty years later. It was not in a newspaper office that I met the impressive looking Robertson Davies, however, but in Massey College, the University of Toronto's new residential graduate college founded in 1963. He was Master of it, and he looked the part.

In the course of his long life as a novelist Robertson Davies wrote more trilogies than I am sure any other novelist in any country has done, three, and he would have completed a fourth had he not had a stroke and died in 1985. The first volume in his first trilogy, the *Salterton* was published in 1951, the second volume of which, *Leaven of Malice* (1954), is one of my favourites. All the volumes in his second trilogy, the *Deptford*, won Robertson Davies great fame – *Fifth Business* (1970), *The Manticore* (1972), which won the Governor-General's Literary Award for a novel in the English language, and *World of Wonders* (1975).

He was well-established when he wrote his third trilogy – *The Rebel Angels* (1981), *What's Bred in the Bone* (1985) and *The Lyre of Orpheus* (1985). I waited eagerly to read his next novel to appear. The incomplete *Toronto* trilogy, well-named, had a well-named second novel, *The Coming Men* (1994). Almost unbelievably prolific, Robertson Davies, who was never called by any other name, was given an Honorary Doctorate of Letters in Oxford in 1991, my last year there, and a year later he became the first Canadian to become an Honorary Member of the American Academy and Institute of Arts and Letters. In 2007 he had a park in Toronto named after him.

I had another link with him. In the 1950s he played a major role in launching the Stratford Shakespearian Festival in Canada, with Tyrone Guthrie as its first Director, and with him published three books on the Festival's early years. Canada's Stratford Festival, which I enjoyed attending, and Tyrone Guthrie personally, had a great influence on the founding of the Chichester Festival in Sussex. I was very active there in its early years, being a friend of Leslie Evershed-Martin who did more to promote the Chichester Theatre than anyone else. He also encouraged me to join the Spectacle Makers' Company, the first Livery Company which I had joined. It had no hall of its own but met in the extremely old and attractive Apothecaries' Company Hall. It had not been damaged during the Second World War.

Nor had any interesting modern buildings in the great city of Toronto on the other side of the Atlantic. In the wake of Robertson Davies comes the great Canadian author Margaret Atwood. I read every novel of hers that I could, some of them deeply disturbing. Margaret Atwood's surname appealed to me before I read any of them.

Thomas Attwood (with two ts) of Birmingham was the first historical figure that I wrote about, and firsts always matter not only in university examinations but in articles and books. Founder of the Birmingham Political Union, which played an important part in the struggle for the Great Reform Bill between 1830 and 1832, Attwood proved a far more interesting figure than I expected when I started my research on him.

As I am finishing the text of this chapter I have just read Margaret Atwood's learned and highly readable *In Other Worlds: SF and the Human Imagination*, published by Virago in 2011, a book that I myself would love to have written. She has just completed a trilogy of her own. It began with a volume that was published in 2001, *Oryx and Crake*, which is set in a weird world that had been devastated by an unnamed catastrophe. The second volume, *The Year of the Flood*, followed six years later. It told the same story as *Oryx and Crake*, not seen as Jimmy and his friend, a bigoted racist codenamed Crake, saw it, but by two women whose lives intertwine with theirs.

Instead of focusing on science, *The Year of the Flood* focuses on religion. A New Age activist group, God's Gardeners, is working with a mysterious network, MaddAddam, and it is this network that gives the title to the third volume in Atwood's trilogy. It draws in minor characters and sub-plots from the first two volumes, and these now provide the main plot. The author turns the full force of what is satire, more than sci-fi, on bioengineered liobams, creatures half-lion half-lamb, and a perverted Church of Petroleum.

When I speculate on the nature of trilogies I bring in what I regard as 'real religion' from the start. I think of the Trinity, three-in-one and One in Three, 'Faith, Hope, Charity [or Love]' and 'Prepare the Way'. *Omne trium perfectum*, 'everything that comes in threes is perfect'. I go on to ponder also on religion and science and topicality and history. These are special relationships which I might have dwelt on more fully in the second volume of this trilogy to which I gave that name. I have lots of loose ends to tie up. Why did I not mention trios once in my chapter on music? Nor did I mention 'Onward Christian Soldiers' or the thrilling pop song turned into a film 'Stand by Me'.

The relationship between film and song is obviously another special relationship. In the last chapter of *Special Relationships*, which I called 'Connections and Convergences', I might have added to these the word coincidences, abundant in Margaret Atwood. I have included 'Coincidences', however, in the penultimate chapter of *Loose Ends and Extras* after 'Words, Links'. It is a deliberately short chapter as is my last chapter which pulls my book together 'Pasts, Present, Futures'.

In concluding the first chapter of *Loose Ends and Extras* I must insist that in writing history it is important neither to exaggerate nor to oversimplify. The processes of thinking are complex. Historians must think in depth and, most important, seek to compare. I do not always think in threes. Some thought is singular, the adjective used by Strachey to describe the Victorian era. Twos and fours and indeed all numbers can figure in thought. I like picking out prime numbers. When and how numbers influence thinking is investigated by Daniel Tammet in *Thinking in Numbers* (2012). Anthropology as well as astronomy and sometimes astrology – the relationship between them is a very special one – come to the aid of historians. Partners are usually two. Monogamy is basic to our culture, but in others so is polygamy. Many threes become fours. I think of history as local, regional, national, but I now have to add global. This is a word which has almost completely changed its meaning and extended its use since I became a professional historian.

Chapter 2

Nineties, Sixties, Thirties

The word age does not figure in the title of this chapter. For once numbers speak louder than words. Yet the chapter is about age and aging, and in it I am not just talking about my own lifetime and the advanced age which I have now reached, but about the ages through which I have been living. I have written a lot about the nineties of various centuries in *Fins de Siècle, How Centuries End, 1400–2000* (1996), which I co-edited with my friend Daniel Snowman. I was responsible for the last two chapters in it on the 1890s and the 1990s. The first of them I called 'Past, Present and Future in Headlines', anticipating the last chapter of *Loose Ends and Extras*; the second I called 'The Final Chapter'.

The quality of historical writing on the 1890s has been high. It was the strength of Holbrook Jackson's memorable survey of the 1890s, which inevitably left much out, that he did not ignore economic and social trends, including market trends in production, publishing and, not least, in advertising. His emphasis on the distinctive combination of vitality and of curiosity which he identified in the 1890s still seems well-judged. There was a 'quickening of the imagination' in many fields, an awakening; this represented 'the realisation not of a purpose but of possibilities'. A similar point had been made by one of the most discussed authors of that decade, Max Nordau, their Jeremiah, whose widely read book *Degeneration* published in 1895, acknowledged the vigour of the confused age that he was holding up for judgment. A century later, John Stokes, in his *In the Nineties* (1989), seeking to observe the 1890s 'from within', shows clearly that much that is associated with the late nineties was already there before 1895, the year of Oscar Wilde's trial and of the publication of Nordau's *Degeneration*. He picks out as an example the neglected year 1893, when a revealing public debate raged about suicide, a topic that must be central in any decade to all talk of death and survival.

It is of course central to the 1990s and my final chapter in *Fins de Siècle*. There can never, of course, be a final chapter for history goes on, although in a book much read in the 1990s, which I criticised in *Fins de Siècle* Francis Fukuyama talked of the end of history, *post histoire*. He was wrong, as news headlines in 2014 daily proclaim. We are now in a new millennium, and in the 1990s more was made of the imminence of that millennium than of the decade leading up to it. In 2014 are we still in the noughties, the not very illuminating label for the previous decade?

I move back to the 1860s, 'an age of equipoise', as my friend Professor W. L. Burn described it, which I was writing about before I reached the 1960s, an age of turbulence, but in many ways the golden age of my own life. So it was for blues singer, writer and critic George Melly, five years younger than me. 'Silly and transient they may have been, but at least they were alive, ticking, and above all, hopeful.' The sixties remain a controversial decade on both sides of the Atlantic. It was Melvin Lasky, editor of the severely intellectual monthly magazine *Encounter*, who coined the phrase Swinging London. Margaret Thatcher described the decade, however, as a period of 'fashionable theories and permissive claptrap' as a result of which 'old values of discipline and restraint were denigrated'. The decade was not all of one piece, but there was no sharp break between the early and late sixties as there had been in the fifties, before and after Suez and the Soviet attack on Hungary.

There were common features in the sixties in the United States, from which many of the new elements in the British sixties came, not least drugs. It has been recognised by American historians that the sixties had a sinister side. They cite the case of 'druggy' Charles

Manson, who claimed to be Jesus and promised his followers that they would become winged elves. In a literary supplement to the *Village Voice* (1988) called *Outta Sight*, subtitled 'The Good, the Bad and the 1960s', a reference to a film, Richard Goldstein believed that in the prosperous precincts of America – and Greenwich Village where the *Voice* was written and published was not one of these – decades moved like merchandise.

On both sides of the Atlantic the year 1968 seemed a kind of climax to what another American writer, Michael Thelwell, called 'a score settling, ass-kicking head-whipping, dues-taking, hypocrisy-exposing, innocence-destroying, delusion-ending year'. Vietnam was influencing the American mood not only in 1968 but much later into the seventies, and the memory of it still persists. In Paris, it was a year of *les événements*, student rioting culminating in the fall of de Gaulle. In Sussex University the wind sometimes blew across the Channel, sometimes across the Atlantic.

In 1996 the British historian Arthur Marwick wrote a book giving a British perspective of the 1960s. He was a professor at the Open University, which was itself one of the products of the 1960s. When I read it, I felt that it did not get the relationship between the fifties and the sixties right. In some respects the sixties began in 1956, the year of Suez and Hungary.

I have not written as much about the sixties as about the thirties, the decade when I was brought up, and the 1830s, the first period which I wrote about as a professional historian. It was ushered in by the Great Reform Bill, re-fashioned by the Chartists and after the accession of Queen Victoria in 1837, could be seen as pointing forward, if not very clearly, to a whole Victorian age. In 2010 Juliet Gardiner wrote a detailed study of the 1930s. I knew Juliet well through publishing and through *History Today*, which she edited from 1981 to 1985. In her preface she writes:

> . . . the thirties is a statement as well as a decade. And it is one
> that is frequently heard today, because while those years are
> gradually slipping from our grasp, what they have come to

represent is ever more present: confusion, financial crises, rising unemployment, scepticism about politicians, questions about the proper reach of Britain's role on the world.

She notes that to W. H. Auden, sitting on a bar stool in New York in September 1939, the thirties were a 'low, dishonest decade'. Looking back later others followed him, labelling it 'the devil's decade', 'a dark tunnel', 'the locust years' and 'a morbid age'. She notes also, however, that this was only 'a partial picture'. It ignored symbols of prosperity during the decade like the growth of home ownership, evidenced by rapidly multiplying semi-detached houses and 'the hope of a baby Austin in the garage'. She calls this J. B. Priestley's new 'third England' to set alongside two old Englands, one the bygone rural England, the second harsh, ugly and industrial. She had begun her preface with three lines from Louis MacNeice's 'Autumn Journal' written in 1939:

> There will be time to audit
> The accounts later, there will be sunlight later
> And the equation will come out at last.

I lived through the decade, but I do not figure in the thirties as described by Juliet Gardiner. Nor does Dylan Thomas, born in 1914. He published his first book, *Eighteen Poems*, in 1934. In *Deaths and Entrances*, published in 1946, he included a poem 'In October' which begins 'It was my thirtieth year to heaven'. Dylan Thomas lived only to his own late thirties. He died at the age of thirty-nine. His centenary is being remembered in 2014 with Dylan Thomas festivities organised by the Welsh Government and the British Council in Wales. Jeff Towns, who runs Dylan's Bookstall in Swansea, has said he was expecting the centenary to reinforce the poet's global reputation as well as provide an economic boost for the region.

There are now far more people who are around my age than there were in 1945. Richard Ingrams, who has just reached 76, is the editor and publisher of *The Oldie* which has reached a circulation of 45,000. According to official statistics the number of Britons aged over 80 will more than double to 6.2 million in 25 years. By 2037, 1 in 12 people will be 80 or over. The number aged over 90 will more than triple, while the number of centenarians will rise more than 9-fold from 13,000 to 111,000.

The title of this chapter, a threesome, is misleading in that it leaves out unborn children. I have read a poem by Ian Underwood called 'Poem of fear for my unborn child'.

The right way to end this chapter seems to me to go back to the eighteenth century. A clergyman, Thomas Secker, living from 1693 to 1768, noted in a sermon 'Mistake not the Beginning of Life for the Whole. Providence in its Great Wisdom has furnished every Period of it with proper Satisfactions of its own.'

I began this chapter in 2013 in my own nineties, an age that I never expected to reach, and so my historical perspectives are quite different from those of people now in their sixties or now in their thirties. We all coexist, but we face difficulties in trying to understand each other. Old and young tend to view each other with more than a touch of suspicion. Thirty years used to be considered, and many people still consider it so, as the span of a generation, and the concept of a generation has shaped people's thinking and feeling about the historical process. Each generation, in the words of Ian Martin, writing in the *Guardian*, draws a curtain around the generation that went before. Martin belongs to what is now being called the baby-boom generation. When the baby-boom was at its height, on the eve of the founding of the University of Sussex, it was already being held to account, along with changes in sixth forms and in the attitudes of girls at school, for the increase in the number of people wishing to go to university. After I arrived in Sussex University I refused to use the words 'the young' generically, as many of my contemporaries did. Sussex undergraduates well under the age of thirty did not like to hear themselves described as such. That was not, however, why I refused to do so.

Chapter 3

Development of the Sciences at Sussex University

A s an undergraduate in Cambridge just before the Second World War began and during the first two years of it I was in a college where the sciences mattered. As a fellow and tutor of an Oxford college just before the Second World War ended and during the ten years after it I was in a college where the sciences barely mattered at all. In a jubilee lecture at the University of Sussex delivered on 8 February 2013 on the invitation of Michael Farthing, its present Vice-Chancellor, I chose as a historian and as the University's second Vice-Chancellor to trace the early development of the sciences in Sussex. Relatively little had been written about them, but more than I knew when Michael invited me. My chapter covers more ground than I covered in my lecture.

The obvious contrasts in my personal experiences that I note at the beginning of the chapter are not unique to me, and there will be far more contrasts to come later in this chapter. Sidney Sussex College was not unique in Cambridge in the range of sciences taught or in the proportion of students reading science subjects. In a room in the Tower behind mine above the entrance to the college were the rooms of a distinguished professor who was a much-consulted world authority on human nutrition. In the room on the staircase immediately opposite mine lived the senior scholar in mathematics. I was the senior scholar in history. Someone had quite deliberately placed us there. The Tower was privileged space.

In the first volume of this trilogy, *Secret Days: Code-breaking at Bletchley Park*, I wrote of the wartime drive to convert 'arts students' into scientists to serve the demands of the war effort. I described there the role of C. P., later Lord Snow in handling the process of conversion. This is how it worked. In my own college the Physics Fellow wished me to go into the radar establishment at Malvern, and after interviewing me in nearby Christ's College on a grey Cambridge day Snow approved of his choice. He told me that my call-up into the Forces due on my twenty-first birthday in 1942 would not take place. I would go to Malvern. He would ensure that this would be so. He could not ensure it, for in the spring of 1942 I was informed by him that Malvern had made such good progress with radar that it no longer needed 'arts graduates'.

This was not, however, the end of my Snow story. When I was lecturing in 2012 in the University of Hong Kong on the occasion of its centenary, I had the pleasure of meeting Snow's son Philip, who has written a thorough and extremely stimulating book, *The Fall of Hong Kong: Britain, China and the Japanese Occupation* (2004). I know Hong Kong well, but in reading it I learned much that I did not know. That was tying up a loose end as I had tied up loose ends with his father when, long after he interviewed me in wartime Christ's College, a college that I got to know well after the war, we discussed his Cambridge novel sequence, *Strangers and Brothers*. The eleventh and last novel in the sequence was called appropriately *Last Things*.

Going back from Christ's College to Sidney Sussex, I knew that in 1939 at the very beginning of the war some of my contemporaries reading mathematics in Sidney had made their way to what was then to me an unknown destination as code-breakers, invited there by the mathematics Fellow of my college, Gordon Welchman, an able organiser as well as a talented mathematician. At last he will be the subject of a book, *Gordon Welchman: Bletchley Park's Architect of Ultra Intelligence*, that will come out before *Loose Ends and Extras*. I am going back both ways door-to-door by car to its launching at

Bletchley Park where I launched the first volume of this trilogy. Some of Welchman's recruits in the early part of the war had not completed their Mathematics Tripos. The senior mathematics scholar, Stephen Betts, was not one of them; he was to become an RAF officer. The mathematics exhibitioner, Howard Smith, was taken by Welchman. He and Stephen were bridge partners. I played against them partnered by my fellow history scholar, John Harrison. I knew Howard Smith well. He was to become better-known through the Foreign Office than through code-breaking.

Another Sidney mathematician, John Herivel, was one of those who went to what I now know was Bletchley Park with Welchman. He was a Northern Irelander and was to prove himself an excellent code-breaker who was to write much about the Park and the Enigma operation after restrictions on writing about them were lifted in the 1970s. A third mathematician who went there was David Rees, who became a professor at Exeter University where one of my grandsons is now a student. David, the most modest of men, sadly died while I was writing *Loose Ends*.

All this sounds complicated, and it remains so to me. I did not know then that my great friend, Jim Passant, the history Fellow, knew all about Bletchley Park and went there from time to time. He was in Intelligence. He never taught me but I got to know and like his wife Audrey and every member of his family. The most extraordinary thing in retrospect was that while eventually I did get into Bletchley Park in 1943 I did not get there by a direct route. When I was called up in 1942 I was posted to the Royal Corps of Signals at Catterick Camp, where I learned about wireless and how to use Morse, and on leaving Catterick I began training to be a wireless interceptor. That was a form of military service that would have interested me.

As it was, I was transferred to the Intelligence Corps, to which I had no desire to move and I had to pass through the Intelligence Corps Depot. It was then located in King Alfred's College which is now the University of Winchester. I was in the Depot long enough to go to the cinema and watch *Gone with the Wind*. When the Corps moved from Winchester to Wentworth Woodhouse, a great eighteenth-century house, near Rotherham, we were not told where we were going, but I very soon realised that the train, a real wartime train into which we were crammed, was taking us further and further north. I knew that I would not be too far from Keighley. To the very end of our journey I did not know exactly where we were. It was in the wartime black-out and all the station and road signs were taken away. Yet in the dark as we were, I and my fellow soldiers were amazed to be welcomed to Rotherham by a brass band playing on the station platform. Once laboriously installed in the stables at Wentworth Woodhouse we very quickly fell asleep. There were some brilliant men, particularly brilliant linguists, a few of whom understood more than thirty languages, some of them very exotic, going through the Depot with me, and we were all subjected to deliberately humiliating drilling by non-commissioned officers from the Guards who despised intelligence. They were bullies.

Once I was through the Intelligence Corps Depot my military career seemed to be following a pre-determined course. I would become a field security officer, and I duly went across to Matlock to follow a field security course. There one of my sergeant instructors, very different from the Guards NCOs at the Depot, was the man who had taught me sixth-form French at Keighley Boys' Grammar School. I seemed to be moving round in circles, not sure whether these too were pre-determined. Yet I knew that I would never be a field security officer after I fell from a tree while taking part in an assault course at Matlock.

When I got back, hobbling, to the Intelligence Corps depot at Wentworth Woodhouse I told a friendly young officer to whom I was attached as a kind of orderly, that I now wanted above all to be employed in some alternative branch of intelligence to field security. He was sympathetic, but it was by my own efforts that I made my way into code-breaking. I was posted to Bedford on a cipher course where students, some of them civilians, were being taught hand ciphers along with some German language. I felt like Bunyan's valiant pilgrim.

The course was agreeable and relaxed and I liked Bedford as a town. In following the course I was not called upon to show the qualities shown by Christian in *Pilgrim's Progress*. Yet I did have companions, and some of the ones that I met on my Bedford course became good friends for the rest of their lives, among them Alec Hyatt King, later head of the Music Library in the British Museum, Alexander Lieven, future head of the BBC's Russian Service, and Edward Boyle, future Secretary of State for Education and eventually Vice-Chancellor of Leeds University. I also met and made good friends who were following an Army-organised Japanese language course in Bedford and it was with them that I celebrated my twenty-first birthday.

While on the Bedford course we heard nothing at all about machine codes. We went far enough back in time to deal with a code dating back to the Spanish Armada. I did know that Gordon Welchman was near at hand in Bletchley Park, but I still had no idea of what he was doing there or what he had done. He was in fact the head of a small team of code-breakers who were regularly breaking messages encrypted on the so-called Enigma machine, the most important German coding device, in Hut Six; and when my Bedford course was over, I was posted into Hut Six just in time to work under Welchman himself. He was about to be moved up by Commander Travis, head of Bletchley Park, to be his Assistant Director for Mechanization.

Once inside Hut Six I found myself working with, among others, people I had known at Sidney Sussex who unlike me had got to the Park by a direct route. On the morning after Britain declared war Welchman arrived with some of them. Once inside the Park I quickly became aware of the complexity of the code-breaking operations. There were code-breakers in some Huts who were breaking hand cyphers and some code-breakers in other Huts who were tackling interesting on-line non-Morse codes. Max Newman, whom Welchman had heard lecture at Cambridge when he was an undergraduate from 1925 to 1928, and Major (later Colonel) Tester were in charge of what were known as the Newmanry and the Testery. They needed Britain's first computer, Colossus, to enable them to break these codes. Members of Hut Six were not supposed to know for various reasons what soldiers and civilians in huts other than our own were doing. For various reasons I knew more than most.

In *Secret Days* I have described my experiences and those of others, the vast majority of them women, working inside Bletchley Park and in its out-stations. Without them and the 'bombes', not computers, which they worked on we could not have won the war. I learned far more in Hut Six (without being taught) than how to break codes. I am glad to say I was participating in the remarkable 'Hut' system that Welchman had perfected – it is not easy to explain briefly just what it was – and I realised, while participating in a 'section' of his Hut Six how good code-breakers could be distinguished from the less good. I learned much, too, about individual motivation, what made people tick, and, most important of all, about teamwork. Bletchley Park depended on cooperating teams. The brilliant people working there could not break codes on their own, although in 1939 a few of them, like Dilly Knox, had thought that they could. They were working in cottages not huts.

I also learned how Hut Six drew in recruits by a direct route from universities and schools. The universities were in Scotland and Wales as well as in England. Not all universities were included, but women were as well as men. In the social circumstances of 1939 to 1945 the schools had to be public schools. Marlborough was outstanding among them, but several other schools knew how to supply Bletchley with pupils with a talent for mathematics. A few public-school boys joined Hut Six directly. Their routes there were as secret as the codes they would break.

I carried these lessons with me after the war when I became a Fellow and Tutor of Worcester College. The second Provost after I arrived, J. C. Masterman, had been in wartime Intelligence himself, though never in code-breaking. He was the one person with whom I could discuss in the quiet of Worcester aspects of what I had been doing during the war inside Bletchley Park. Yet I learned more of what he himself had been doing in his fascinating double-cross work than he learned or cared to learn about what I had been doing as a code-breaker.

As far as college matters were concerned, Masterman had not the slightest interest in the sciences. Nor did he think that I had. He put me in charge of a new finance committee. Nevertheless he knew more about public schools, their headmasters and the abilities of their teachers and in what subjects they specialised than any other Oxford head of a college. It was secret knowledge. He was only just behind the scenes in many key school appointments, and he knew just which appointments were key, not only those of headmasters but men who would eventually become headmasters. His was a completely male world. Nevertheless he accepted my help in offering him a share, with her approval, in my female secretary's time and later in his life and mine gave me a courteous welcome when in 1976 I returned as Provost.

There was then only one science lecturer in Worcester, a pleasant young biologist, not a Fellow, who delighted the Dean of the College, Cyril Wilkinson, head of the University Officer Training Corps, before, during and after the war. Wilkinson, who engineered Masterman's appointment – although he would never have used that verb – liked to ask the young biologist questions on every science, including both chemistry and physics, and he expected him to answer them. To please the Dean, who was almost grotesquely ignorant of all the sciences, the young biologist patiently did so, answering question after question, however absurd.

Other Fellows were silent, but one Professorial Fellow, H. J. Seddon, talked with me quietly and in secret about the future of sciences in the college. We both knew that for any college to be without any science Fellows was a grim prospect. Seddon, born in 1903, was much older than me and seemed quite alone. The one Fellow in Medicine in the College, John Walker, was a friend of mine, although we talked more about literature than about the sciences, and I was excited when a lively and witty Catalan Professor, Joseph Trueta, was attached to the college as Nuffield Professor of Orthopaedic Surgery in 1949, succeeding Seddon. Unlike Seddon, he had a strong sense of fun which I only slowly came to know studying science often fostered.

I found this sense of fun at its extreme in the writing of the brilliant American physicist Richard P. Feynman, who was studying physics in Princeton when, still without a doctoral degree, he moved west to

Los Alamos in the New Mexico desert to work on the Manhattan Project, the making of the world's first atomic bomb. That was the place to which Robert Oppenheimer moved too as Director. Feynman greatly admired him. I got to know Oppenheimer well, or as well as it was possible to do, when I was a Fellow of the Institute for Advanced Study. He always kept a lot in reserve.

Two years before the United States entered the war following Pearl Harbor, Feynman had felt that he should make a contribution to the allied war effort before his country joined in, and he asked a friend what he should do. The friend suggested that he should see a colonel in the Army Signal Corps, and the colonel told Feynman in plain language that what he should do was to go to the Corps camp and undertake basic training. 'Wasn't there some way in which his talent could be used more directly?', Feynman asked. 'No' was the answer. 'This is the way the Army is organised. Go through the regular way.' That was what I was expected to do in England after my radar way ahead had been for good reasons closed to me.

Feynman was the American physicist most admired by the theoretical physicist Roger Blin-Stoyle whom I personally welcomed into the Sussex University community on Oxford station in 1961 and who worked with me very closely indeed in the years when I was Pro-Vice-Chancellor. Together we prepared logistics of development papers covering student numbers and faculty requirements. The first of them was dated 23 October 1962. The very language we used was unusual then in universities. Curiously the University's first Vice-Chancellor, an Oxonian, John Fulton, at first still called Principal, the title he had had at Swansea, had asked me to be his deputy, the Pro-Vice Chancellor, on Brighton station as my train was moving out. Once Roger and I arrived at the University, John left all logistic planning of student and faculty numbers to the two of us. I never once heard him use the word logistics.

In the period of office of my successor, Denys Wilkinson, himself a physicist from Oxford, where for fourteen years he had been building up the University's largest science laboratory, Roger edited an indispensable book, published by John Spiers, to mark the silver jubilee of the University. It was called *The Sussex Opportunity: A New University*, and the co-editor was Geoff Ivey, who had been Personal Assistant to me when I was Vice-Chancellor. I learned for the first time from the preface to this book that before I welcomed Roger on Oxford railway station he had actually applied for the post of Professor of Theoretical Physics at Sussex. He had just spent a sabbatical year at the Massachusetts Institute of Technology, a great institution which I knew well, and back in Oxford felt frustrated by 'the sluggishness of the wheels of change' there.

By 1986, when he co-edited *The Sussex Opportunity* and asked me to write a chapter for him, I was back in Worcester College as Provost, a post I never applied for. I confess that while I was happy to be back in a college that I loved, I often felt more frustrated once there than I had ever been at Sussex. The Fellows of the college had changed far less than I had, and although there was now an engineering Fellow, Ray Franklin, long since retired, with whom I am still in contact in 2014, and three science Fellows, I was never asked by any Fellow of the college what my Sussex years had been like except for how I had dealt with radical students. I made it my mission as Provost to broaden the range of science subjects taught in the college, beginning with geology (for which I secured outside funds through an old pupil of mine) and to increase the number of science and engineering Fellows. My happiest year was when the Physics Fellow, Ian Aicheson, whom I had picked out as Senior Tutor, told me that every one of the year's physics undergraduates had got a First. Terrific!

I did my best to persuade the science Fellows in the college to take on college posts. They did not like it, but a few, like Ian, did and served the college in various capacities. Ian was a wonderful college tutor. In a quite different capacity Arthur Dexter became a helpful Wine Steward. Looking back, I feel there were too many College committees and not enough of a sense of individual initiative.

There were certainly too many in Sussex. In what I believe is a revealing essay in *The Sussex Opportunity*, which I wrote a decade after I had left Sussex, I went over the whole of my period as Vice-Chancellor, recalling and re-assessing what I had attempted and achieved. It was given a misleading title, not by me, 'The Years of Plenty, 1967–76', doubtless to contrast those years with the years covered in the next chapter 'The Lean Years', which spanned the then incomplete years of Vice-Chancellor Wilkinson, my successor. My years were never really years of plenty in the University. At best there was relative plenty.

While we were granted funds by the UGC to put up 'arts' and science buildings, we had no UGC funds to run and to plan a working campus on a chalk site, permeable limestone, which linked a new university with the world 55 million years ago, 'new' and 'old' with a vengeance. I wanted the campus to generate a community. It needed roads, lighting, car parks and much else. They too needed planning and we had an efficient Planning Committee which included some students and some members of Council as well as members of Faculty.

The planning procedures set out in the logistics of development papers by Roger and me were far in advance of the then relatively unsophisticated planning procedures of the UGC itself, and so was our planning of buildings and services. Procedures are, of course, instrumental, and principles and objectives have to be clearly stated as they were explicitly at Sussex. Both procedures and principles are at the core of any effective strategy. I learned that from business, and I had benefited immensely from the fact that when I was a member of the UGC there were businessmen of calibre, like Geoffrey Heyworth, Chairman of Unilever, as well as academics serving on it.

I went on many fascinating UGC visitations, a pompous word, to universities in England, Scotland and Wales, where I met the Vice-Chancellor, academic staff (faculty was not then a term in use in most of them), students and members of Council. The last entirely happy UGC visitation to Sussex in my time was on 18 January 1966 before I became Vice-Chancellor. In December 1973, the last UGC visitation in my time was entirely unhappy. There had been a delayed quinquennial settlement that fell short not only of the University's hopes but of its expectations. The UGC itself was short of government funds, having received far less from the government than it had calculated was necessary to carry out its public responsibilities.

That was not, however, the worst of the problems for Sussex. Before the members of the UGC visited our campus they had not fully acquainted themselves with the distinctive pattern of studies at Sussex and they were not in a position, therefore, to ask knowledgeable questions of us. It was abundantly clear to me, however, that it was not just that they found our procedures as inconvenient for them as we found answering their questionnaires. They did not like the principles that we had followed during the 1960s and 1970s in seeking to make Sussex a distinctive university. That was what the then UGC Chairman, Sir Keith Murray, later Lord Murray, and his members wanted it to be before we took in any students either in the arts or sciences.

As a member of the UGC myself, appointed in 1959, when I was still a Professor at Leeds University, and serving on it until 1967, when I became Vice-Chancellor of Sussex, I knew at first hand just what Keith and the members had had in mind. I was particularly close to two of my fellow members, Sir Eric, later Lord, Ashby, to whom I talked a lot about the biological sciences and his illuminating little book *Technology and the Academics*, and to Sir Willis Jackson, an engineer at Imperial College, who had strong views on the state of engineering teaching in the universities which I shared with him. He in turn shared my views about attempting to bring together sciences, arts and social sciences.

I have moved far across time in order to see the issues and events of the 1960s in perspective, something that all historians must do, whatever the issues and events that concern them. I now return somewhat chastened to the 1960s in order to recapture what we were dreaming of and actually achieving in the five years between the arrival of the first science students in 1962 and my becoming Vice-Chancellor in 1967. They were exciting and challenging years, with no two years the same. Annual variations in the numbers of arts and science students changed the mood of the university. Some newly appointed members of Faculty, specialists in their own fields, did not understand our own unique university structure.

In Fred Gray's handsome and beautifully illustrated book *Making the Future: A History of the University of Sussex* (2012), which celebrates, as I do, the fiftieth anniversary of the founding of the University, the 'Overview: doing science' has perspectives totally different from mine and those of my colleagues in 1967. It starts with the sentence 'Sussex in the 1980s was one of the leading places where the study of man as a thinking, feeling, perceiving and active being was thriving.' The perspectives of the authors of this overview were bound to be different from mine. Neither of its two authors arrived in Sussex until the 1980s. I am thinking as I write of the University, a much smaller university, twenty years before.

The fact that I was not myself a scientist in the years that I am writing about in this chapter does not, in my view, handicap me as I tell a genuinely inside story. When I was in the fifth form at Keighley Boys' Grammar School and took what was then called my Matriculation examination, chemistry was my best subject and the senior chemistry master, nicknamed 'Fatty Acid', called at my home to tell me of my matric results before they were officially announced. He wanted me to take chemistry as a subject for my advanced level. If I were at school now in 2014 I would most likely be placed on the 'science side' before going on to university.

Even in the late 1930s more boys from KBGS went on to study chemistry at university than any other subject. The reason why it was never a serious option for me was that I had a historian headmaster, a man of total determination who would never have allowed me to study any other subject but history or to study it in any other place than his own old college, Sidney Sussex. Not surprisingly, since my parents who knew nothing about universities backed him totally, I followed him there. I knew that he had my long-term future in mind and that he strongly cared.

Most KBGS students of the 1930s who were intending to read the sciences were sent to St John's College, Cambridge, and it was a surprise for me when I got to Sidney Sussex to discover that more undergraduates there were studying science subjects than history. I got on well with them at Sidney Sussex where I was a member not only of the venerable Confraternitas Historica, with which I have always stayed in touch, but of the Argonauts, a society which brought together scientists and non-scientists and has long since disappeared.

There had been a science strand in the experience of my own family, essentially practical science, and my grandfather, Abraham, born in Leeds, who after apprenticeship became an artisan engineer, had read, kept and in old age passed on to me a little book he had bought in 1872 called *Introduction to the Sciences*. This covered, in an age before specialisation transformed learning, a very wide range of subjects, astronomy, 'natural philosophy' (in other words non-laboratory based physics), geology and physical geography, meteorology, electricity and magnetism, chemistry, the most important of the sciences in Victorian England, botany, zoology, human physiology, and 'mental philosophy'.

I was excited by this little book and treasure my copy of it. It is my frontispiece illustration to *Loose Ends*. I know that as a young man my grandfather was as well-informed about politics as he was about the sciences. He had gone up from Leeds to London after finishing his apprenticeship where he listened to Gladstone give a public speech. He also ate his first tomatoes there, not knowing what they were. He thought they were fruit to eat in the streets. Back from London, he then moved from Leeds to Barrow-in-Furness where, like my father who followed after him, he held a highly responsible post in Vickers-Armstrong. My father, William, was interested in politics as Abraham had been. Yet the older Abraham got, the more fascinated he became not by politics but by history, ancient, medieval and modern, a very familiar threesome.

Biology did not figure among the subjects treated in the *Introduction to the Sciences* which he gave to me. Nevertheless, it was the biological sciences which drew me to science two years before I left Leeds for Sussex in 1959. This was the centenary year of the publication of Charles Darwin's *Origin of Species*, and during the course of it I took part in a number of symposia and wrote papers and reviews about Darwin and his personal evolution. My interest grew in the 1960s and 1970s, and when, in December 2007, the present Vice-Chancellor of Sussex, Michael Farthing, first approached me to give my jubilee lecture the first title that I thought of giving to it was 'Origin of Science at Sussex'. I was not sure, however, that my audience would grasp the historical cross-reference.

I knew, however, that they would be as interested as I was in the origins of one crucial word in this chapter, 'scientist'. Fortunately its usage has been studied meticulously and admirably recorded by Sidney Ross in his *Nineteenth Century Attitudes: Men of Science*, published in the Netherlands in 1991. This was based on articles that Ross had published previously elsewhere, the first of them in 1962 in *Annals of Science*. Coincidentally that was the year when the first science students arrived in Sussex.

The word scientist was first used in the *Quarterly Review* for March 1834. Reviews were then anonymous, but we know that this review was written by William Whewell, who went on to become Master of Trinity College, Cambridge. He also coined many other new scientific words, including physicist. The word science itself was, of course, much older, as was the adjective scientific. By the late 1820s Thomas Carlyle, reviewing anonymously in the great Whig rival of the *Quarterly Review*, the *Edinburgh Review*, had called it a 'sign of the times' that 'on all sides it was recognised that the Metaphysical and Moral Sciences' were 'falling into decay' while 'the Physical [were] engrossing, every day, more respect and attention'.

Between 1829 and 1834 the first national British conferences on the sciences outside the Royal Society, those of the British Association for the Advancement of Science, were held in York, Oxford and Cambridge. Whewell referred to the first of them in his review, noting, as he had done at York, a 'tendency' of the sciences to 'separation' and 'dismemberment'. 'The mathematician turns away from the chemist, the chemist from the naturalist.' Thus, science, even more physical science, 'loses all traces of unity'. There was no general term by which 'the gentlemen' at York could describe themselves with reference to their pursuits.

Whewell proposed, therefore, that 'by analogy with artist' they might employ the word 'scientist'. It would be no more contentious than 'economist' or 'atheist'. He was wrong to assume this. From the start the two words scientist and physicist were highly controversial, and they remained so even sixty years later in 1894 when professionalism was entering university science as it was entering non-university sport. Thus, the editor of *Science Gossip*, the tempting title of a new journal designed for students of science, wrote in that year that the application of the word scientist was 'not satisfactory'. It was 'usually the offspring of a paucity of erudition and expression which comes of the modern system of cramming with text-books and general hurry in education'.

T. H. Huxley (1825–95) was even more damning. He was one of eight prominent public figures approached by the editor of *Science Gossip* to give their views on nomenclature. 'To anyone who respects the English language . . . "scientist" must be about as pleasing a word as "electrocution". I sincerely trust you will not allow the pages of *Science Gossip* to be defiled by it.' Huxley, who coined the word 'agnostic' – he would have been surprised by Whewell's choice of 'atheist' as an example – was an influential public figure in the development and professionalisation of Victorian science. He had a wide circle of influential friends and sat on innumerable commissions and committees. He was reckoned an outstanding chairman not only of committees but of public meetings. Yet he has passed into history mainly as Charles Darwin's bulldog. He is the subject of a magnificent two-volume biography by Adrian Desmond, which I strongly recommend. Volume One, published in 1994, was called *The Devil's Disciple*, Volume Two, published in 1997, *Evolution's High Priest*. He would have been shocked by both titles as he would have been by Cyril Bibby's *T. H. Huxley: Scientist [sic], Humanist and Educator* (1959). Desmond's two volumes are now conveniently available in a single Penguin paperback.

Alfred Russell Wallace, only two years older than Huxley, who propounded evolution as natural selection in the same year as Darwin, 1859, was able to offer *Science Gossip* his opinions on the use of the word scientist, which he wrongly thought to be American in origin. They were very different from Huxley's. 'As we have Biologist, Zoologist, Botanist, Chemist, Physicist, Physiologist and Specialist, why should we not use "Scientist"? As the Americans say, it has come to stay.' Wallace has left behind a two-volume autobiography and a fascinating book, *The Wonderful Century*, which investigates the gains and losses in the century in which he was born and lived.

It was left to a surviving gentleman-scientist, not an academic but an aristocrat, the Duke of Argyll, Huxley's sworn enemy, whom he tried to bruise whenever he spoke and wrote of him, to argue that: 'All the so-called sciences are applications of philosophy to particular regions . . . They ought still to be called natural philosophy.' It was sad that some of the teachers of philosophy in Cambridge University talked then of 'scientists' – 'preposterous word!' – and opposed them to 'philosophers' as though they were 'cats and dogs who are bound to fight when they meet'.

Here is my own sting in the tail. When I was talking very seriously to my friend Stephen Toulmin about coming to Sussex University in the mid-1960s I was talking to a scholar whom I had met in Leeds University when he was Professor of Philosophy there. The adjective natural did not figure in his designation. I had the unique experience at Sussex of being about to tell the Senate that he was coming to join us when the Registrar passed a note to me that he had decided not to come. Toulmin was going instead to join the Committee of Social Thought in Chicago University

I was not entirely surprised. Stephen quickly became a lifelong friend. He would not have been surprised when we were both at Leeds University that I did not consult him when I introduced in the School of History a pioneering course on the history of scientific thought as an alternative course to the history of political thought, standard in most universities, and the history of economic thought, less common. This was a threesome, but unlike PPE a threesome within which a student had to choose one kind of thought only.

I now realise that my six years at Leeds, a red-brick university with a great and forward-looking medical school, a large number of science and engineering students and a correspondingly large number of academics teaching them, were not only important in hardening my objections to departmentalism but in encouraging me to look for opportunities for change. What I accomplished there directly influenced what I was to do in Sussex. Alfred Nissan, Research Professor of Wool Textile Engineering, I admired because he saw the relevance of what he was doing in textile engineering for medical research.

I had nothing to do with the first appointments to the science faculty in Sussex, however, and this made me particularly happy to see a significant number of them present when I gave my jubilee lecture in February 2013. One faculty member of the foundation School of Physical Science, Douglas Brewer, a low-temperature physicist, was the first Sussex scientist apart from Roger Blin-Stoyle whom I got to know as a friend. We have had many interesting links since 1962. We visit each other's houses and talk over and recall not only University of Sussex matters but also Leonard Woolf and Trekkie Parsons and Douglas's brother, a Professor of English Literature, whom I had met quite independently and who became Master of Emmanuel College, Cambridge.

Another Sussex University scientist, David Smith, to whom I owe a debt in writing this chapter, has collected quite remarkable details of the university's chemistry faculty. They were a team bonded together by Colin Eaborn, a chemist from Leicester University to whom the university owes a very special debt. Along with an initially small chemistry contingent, consisting of Eric Peeling, Richard Jackson, Alan Pidcock, Colin Banwell and David James, they started a chemistry major in the School of Physical Sciences, which until 1965 was the only school of science. Eric Peeling was particularly concerned with laboratory design, an obligatory concern of experimental scientists, and from its very beginning the University depended also on non-faculty scientific staff who were organising and developing the laboratories. They were in a ratio of 5 to 4 against the science faculty and dedicated to their work.

They were also very loyal to the university which employed them, and when the historian A. J. P. Taylor in his role as a journalist wrote an article in the *Sunday Express* asserting that at Sussex we were 'living on the fat of the land' and 'swilling down port', the non-faculty scientists wrote complaining of gross misrepresentation. The *Sunday*

Express did not print their letter. I wrote to Taylor myself, whom I admired as a historian, telling him that I myself had never had one glass of port at Sussex up to the time when my attention was drawn to his article, and I confess that I did not get much of a response myself. I think that when he first heard of Sussex he would have liked to become a Professor of History there. He never, as far as I am aware, showed any interest in science.

I know now that before the science members of the then only Science School took up their posts they met and talked over their ideas and plans at the Old Ship Inn in Brighton. Just what they discussed I do not know. I feel sure, however, that they contemplated a bigger university in the years ahead. Within four years, because of growing numbers of science students and science faculty, four new schools were to be created. In 1965, a very special year in the early history of science at Sussex, four new schools emerged from the original single school of science. MOLS, the School of Molecular Sciences, headed by Colin Eaborn, seemed established from the start, and MAPS, Mathematical and Physical Sciences, was a logical extension of the foundation school. BIOLS, Biological Sciences, and APPS, Applied Sciences, were genuinely new.

The UGC, of which I was then a member, had not approved of the start of Applied Sciences in Sussex. Keith Murray, its energetic chairman, who was to become Lord Murray of Newhaven, was not alone in thinking of Sussex as a totally non-industrial region. I myself spent a lot of time going round the county trying to persuade local business-men to give financial support to the School of Applied Sciences and did not raise a penny. Local employers were no more interested in such a school at Sussex than was the UGC.

The School was to flourish nonetheless under the deanship of John West, who arrived from Belfast, and renamed it Engineering and Applied Sciences. Soon the UGC came to support him, and he tried to secure the support of the Wolfson Foundation also. The person I knew best in the School – and he belonged to more than one School – was Robert Cahn, whom I had discovered on a UGC visit to Wales. I liked the very sound of Robert's subject, Materials Science, and recognised its interdisciplinarity. John West, a good and loyal friend, was to leave Sussex when he became Vice-Chancellor of Bradford.

Whatever the limits to the number of industrial products made or bought and sold in the county we were certainly having considerable success in the University in producing Vice-Chancellors. John Kingman, a brilliant mathematician, who married a distinguished Sussex historian, was to become Vice-Chancellor of Bristol. John Scott, a statistician, was to move to a new university in Melbourne, Australia. I met him next at a lively Commonwealth Vice-Chancellors' Conference when we visited several Australian universities, including the Australian National University in Canberra. It was there that I delivered on 2 November 1960 what has become the best-known of all my lectures, 'The Map of Learning'.

While preparing *Loose Ends and Extras* I rediscovered the letter from students at the Australian National University, all of them graduates, asking me to deliver the first Annual Lecture of the Research Students' Association. My lecture was frequently reprinted in Britain with significant additions and modifications, but it is the Australian text, recorded before the University of Sussex existed, which is usually quoted. I took the map image from Francis Bacon, although I quoted a contemporary writer whom I admired, Michael Polanyi, who observed that while the traveller equipped with a detailed map of a region across which he plans his itinerary enjoys a striking practical superiority over an explorer who has no map, nonetheless the explorer's fumbling progress is a richer achievement than the well-briefed traveller's journey.

The footnoted text in David Daiches's book *The Idea of a New University* was published after I had arrived back in England from Australia and had been appointed as Pro-Vice-Chancellor of Sussex. It was, indeed, after the first science faculty and students had arrived. This is recognised explicitly in the British version, which stated correctly that in 1961 the Dean of the School of Physical Sciences, the first Science School, had not yet been appointed and that discussions about the shape of the science curriculum took place only after Roger Blin-Stoyle had taken up the post.

Roger wrote an interesting and revealing chapter in Daiches's book, which was published in 1964, describing these discussions, stressing how important it was to make changes in curricula, teaching methods and research procedures while they could be effected easily. 'The University is still small and flexible, and every advantage must be taken of this in order to iron out inconsistencies and to rectify mistakes.' This judgement implies that there would be inconsistencies and mistakes. There was, however, a unifying vision. The task of Sussex as the first of Britain's new universities was to educate 'a complete scientist'. Understanding was the key word in his formulation. How phenomena were first understood and then described in terms of processes and structures at a more fundamental level needed to be developed in a complete scientist. If Roger had read carefully my Canberra lecture he might have incorporated the idea of exploration. It should be incorporated in his idea of a 'complete scientist'.

Both Roger and I drew attention to the influence of the biological sciences in the scientific map of learning. To me they were the most exciting sciences of the 1960s after the discovery of DNA and the double helix. Moreover some of the most fundamental discoveries made were interdisciplinary. Curiously John Maynard Smith did not treat them as such in the chapter he wrote for the book which Roger edited in 1986 for the twenty-fifth anniversary of Sussex. He concentrated more on experimental psychology and the arrival in Sussex of Stuart Sutherland, a very remarkable and very eccentric Professor of Experimental Psychology. I used to like going down to his home in a fine house in Brighton to talk of free will and risk. When he came into my office at the university he warned me forcefully not to take any academic risks: 'Asa, be quite sure that you never appoint anybody to a professorship who is second-rate. Also be very careful about appointing any professors of psychology at all.' Wise advice. I was very glad that Stuart Sutherland, when cognitive studies were being developed, was followed by Christopher Longuet-Higgins who brought with him to Sussex his Edinburgh team of biologists. I knew Christopher through the BBC, of which he was a Governor, and I was thrilled when he told me he chose to hold his Royal Society Fellowship at Sussex rather than Edinburgh.

The School of Biological Sciences I had dreamed of in Australia. I found biological sciences exciting, to use a cliché at the frontiers of knowledge, and increasingly interdisciplinary, and when I got back I met Jim Danielli, then a professor at King's College, London, who encouraged my thinking about the biological sciences. He would have been my first choice as Dean. Instead he was lured to the United States, leaving us free to choose John Maynard Smith, a professor at University College, London. John had every qualification. He was a graduate in engineering as well as zoology. He was a marvellous lecturer. He took a genuine interest in all his students. He insisted on teaching his first-year students in the way that tutors in arts subjects taught theirs. He easily established links with other parts of the University. He welcomed new initiatives from faculty people who were already in Sussex and attracted new faculty who wanted to join us.

When John Maynard Smith arrived from London and John Morrell arrived from Sheffield, they opened up a whole new era in science at Sussex, wittily described in a short book by John, which I had not read when I started to write this chapter, I thought it wise to recall what the sciences were like before that new era began. I turned back by luck to the twenty-first number of the *University of Sussex Bulletin*, then edited by Jack Lively with Debbie Epstein as student editor. Its first pages were devoted to colloquia and seminars, listed in alphabetical order so that chemistry came first and mathematics before physics. I was particularly glad to see that on page 6 two sets of coming Arts–Science films were announced. The first was a 25-minute Nuffield Foundation film *The God Within*, a study of pre-Socratic philosophy. The second was a 35-minute film, *Cosmos*, a film made in East Germany which presented a biography of Humboldt, described as an eighteenth-century scientist but who was far more than that. The third was a nine-minute Rank film, *Introduction to Feedback*, and the fourth was a thirteen-minute film *Ariel, the first International Satellite*, made by the American Central Office of Information. The fact that the makers of these four films were living under totally different regimes was testimony to the University's care to be judged 'open to all'. I do not know what the feedback referred to in the short Rank film was, or what was the Sussex feedback to it.

The second series of Arts–Science films was equally far-ranging in its origins. *Wave Behaviour* was produced by Bell Laboratories in the USA, 'showing similarities in many aspects of physics'. The second, *The Revealing Eye*, showed 'the capabilities of photography'. How far, I now ask, did it look ahead to what has been one of the biggest advances of my lifetime? The third, *Semiconductors*, recording one of the big transformations of the period, was made in Czechoslovakia, and the fourth was *Vive la Différence*, a tempting title, although I don't know what that particular *différence* was! For the summer term viewers were offered a silent film of 1925 which attempted to demonstrate in cartoon fashion the principles of relativity, a Russian film on illusions seen during space flights, and two of a series by McGraw-Hill, American publishers with world-wide ambitions, that dealt with psychology.

I have no idea who chose these programmes. Was it Martin Brown who developed the Arts–Science scheme in which I took profound interest? I saw him regularly when we looked at degrees of involvement of students in the scheme. It appeared that science students were making far more of it than arts students. Some of them wrote lively dissertations which I read. One was on the songs and music of Bob Dylan, another on the ruins of Lewes priory.

I knew that both science and arts students watched films shown by the University film society, which that term showed *Citizen Kane*, and attended University Lectures, always given capital letters. The names of the lecturers giving them make me feel that I want to go far back in time and listen to what they had to say. Lionel Trilling, whom I got to know in Aspen, when I took part in an almost too lively seminar on 'What is an educated person?', lectured in Sussex on 'Literature and the Modern University', George Woodcock, Secretary of the TUC, the most gloomy trade unionist I have ever met, on 'Trades Unions', Eric Hobsbawm, who needs no introduction to readers, on 'The Industrial History of Culture', and Basil Spence (who better?) on 'Architecture'.

The *Bulletin* also included a fascinating article by the American sociologist David Riesman, then at the height of his powers and influence, on his first impressions of the University of Sussex. I had had no difficulty in persuading Dave to spend his sabbatical leave in Sussex. He had turned down Oxford and, I believe, Cambridge. While with us he did not live on the campus but in the Metropole Hotel in Brighton, and I feared that he would return to Harvard with the draft of a book on the sociology of hotels in his satchel not a book on new universities. His article in the *Bulletin* had been commissioned by Jack Lively, who wanted him to write it before the novelty of being in a new university wore off.

Riesman, who was never to write a book either on the sociology of hotels or of universities, began with the architecture of the University and with Basil Spence. There was nothing pastiche about his Sussex buildings, he wrote. They had nothing in common with the fake Gothic or fake Georgian new university buildings to be seen in the United States. They were even more spectacular than the photographs of them that he had seen before he came. Spacious and inventive, they expressed 'something almost mischievous', an adjective I have never seen elsewhere in descriptions of Spence's work. Nevertheless, it seemed to Riesman that Sussex for its present and immediately fore-seeable future was 'a bit too spread out'. (Would he, if he were able, want to change 'a bit' to 'a lot'?) 'On a cold, damp afternoon there could be a loneliness about the handful of stalking grey figures with everyone else holed up in Brighton.'

Moving from buildings to curriculum, Riesman noted that Sussex had 'taken advantage of openness to attempt some very demanding and intricate curricular experiments in the nearly intractable efforts to bridge the two cultures'. No one could have called him a convert to it. He listed his conclusions frankly. 'Students are likely to seek easier and more closed identities and to fear the amorphousness and ambiguity of the Sussex non-pattern.' His last word still pulls me up with a jerk. As I explained in the first chapter, pattern is a favourite word of mine. If Riesman wanted a new university where there was no overall pattern but strong departments with able and powerful professors at the head of each of them, Warwick University had them in 1965, and I urged Riesman to go and look at it.

I always saw Warwick as being at the opposite end of the new university spectrum from us. I had sympathy with its rebellious students who in its first year complained, in E. P. Thompson's words, that it was Warwick University Limited, a university controlled by local business, but I frankly told my own students at one of the regular meetings I had with them that I had no desire to intervene in the affairs of Warwick or indeed any other university. I refused to condemn Warwick University's first Vice-Chancellor, Jack Butterworth, 'Jolly Jack', later Lord Butterworth, whom I had known years before as a college bursar in Oxford. He was a friend. I had enough to do managing one university, I told them, without taking on a second one.

In the late 1960s I had my own problems with students, although they never wore me down, and when in 1970 I gave a learned lecture on the centenary of the Education Act of 1870 I chose the MOLS building as my place to give it. It was a circular building beautifully simple and rightly now listed. Its lecture theatre was used for a wide range of lectures by insiders and outsiders, including the Vice-Chancellor. I had a row of distinguished people from outside the University sitting in the front row and high up in the rear angry students seeking to discuss not past history but the radical topic of the day, student files. I told them that after I had given my lecture I would open the meeting up to a discussion of what to do about them.

The students listened, if unwillingly, to what I had to say about W. E. Forster, an MP for Bradford, brother-in-law of Matthew Arnold, who laid down in his 1870 Act the first general framework of elementary education for boys and girls up to the age of twelve. It was a great but controversial achievement. I admit the students were not as attentive listeners as my audience in the front row. When I had finished my lecture, which I knew was a good one – I always know when they are, and they are always without notes – I took off my jacket to the surprise of my front row and listened to all that the students had to say.

I ended the evening in MOLS promising to go out into the night and continue discussion elsewhere, with a smaller group including the President of the Students' Union. We very quickly reached an acceptable deal. No one could have access to a student file other than the student whose file it was. There was to be no resort to solicitors or the law. I could then quietly and without fuss draw my own comparisons between the Sussex solution and what other universities were doing. In some of them there were students' strikes about files which lasted for months.

Turning back to the 1965 *Bulletin*, which had no equivalent in other universities, there was one other article of considerable interest in it relevant to this chapter 'Physicists and Interviewing'. It was written by DG (why did he use only his initials?), a member of our Physics faculty who discussed typical questions asked of applicants being interviewed for a student place in physics at Sussex. His first example was 'How do you know that it isn't an electrical force rather than a gravitational one that holds the moon in its orbit?' Silence, he said, usually ensued, and he wondered why he was spending half a day of his valuable time asking such questions – 'and more reasonable ones' – throughout what was probably the busiest term of the year for himself and for students who had been admitted.

Those of his fellow physicists who tutored first-year students had taken a poll of their students' opinions. 'Do you think you were influenced in deciding whether to come to Sussex by the interview rather than by the building and the site?' One third of a hundred students polled said, to the surprise of most of the faculty, that they were. This poll result influenced but did not determine future university entrance procedures. Nine out of ten physics faculty favoured a scheme whereby only two days each year, the first in the second week in December, the second in the second week of the following January, would be devoted to interviewing applicants. Eventually all admissions were to be handled by the University Admissions Office.

By then the pressure on places had been drastically reduced. The number of applications had fallen dramatically. Sussex did not have the same unique appeal, and the national demographic bulge was over.

The time would come when we would have to go out to schools and look for students in all the sciences. From the start, the Professor of Mathematics, Bernard Scott, and his colleague Walter Ledermann, had travelled through the country looking for mathematics students in very different places. Mathematics, the Queen of the Sciences, consequentially had more students in the early years of the University. Walter Ledermann was to long outlive Bernard Scott and was an invaluable member of faculty. Fortunately in the 1960s and early 1970s we were introducing new interdisciplinary academic groupings, such as cognitive studies, which had a real appeal to applicants.

From what I have written it is abundantly clear that on the eve of the substitution of four Science Schools for one in 1965 the university was a lively, indeed exciting place to be for students reading science. I knew too that in 1965 it was also a far more political place to be working than it had been in 1961 and 1962. I did not need the *Bulletin* to tell me that. I knew, too, that there were members of faculty who had strong political views. They included some, but far from all, of the science faculty. One who was, Brian Easly, was a mathematical physicist who in 1973 was to publish *Liberation and the Aims of Science* with the Sussex University Press which had not been brought into existence in 1965.

That was a year after Harold Wilson had won power at the general election of 1964 but was under attack from the left. There was growing concern about what was happening far outside Britain. 'What is happening in Vietnam?' was the question posed in the title of a 1965 lecture given at Sussex by the Lecturer in Vietnamese in London University.

A week later there was a forum in the university on 'the obstacles to cooperation between Communist and Western democratic societies' – 'Are they mythical or insuperable?' The speakers were Ms Y. Crestincic of the Yugoslav newspaper *Politica*, Mr Berezowski of the Polish newspaper *Tribuna Luda* and Mr L. Lederer of *The Observer*. There was now a revived CND Committee in the University, a visiting speaker gave a lecture on CND under the Labour government, and a march in Brighton was announced, sponsored by CND and other bodies. Sussex students took part in a three-day national march, starting in High Wycombe and ending in Trafalgar Square.

To complete the political picture the *Bulletin* announced that the University's Conservative Association was putting on two lectures, one by Timothy Raison, editor of *New Society*, a non-political journal for which I regularly wrote reviews and sometimes articles, and one by the Rt. Hon. Enoch Powell, who had not then made the rivers of blood speech against immigration which led to his dismissal from the shadow cabinet. Powell, then best known for his National Health policies, had contested the leadership of the party with Edward Heath in the year that Sussex's University Conservative Association invited him to speak.

As Pro-Vice-Chancellor in a turbulent time I had to know a lot about politics, mainly left-wing but right-wing too. I was lucky in having been a Tutor in Politics in Worcester College. The body that I was most proud of at Sussex, the Science Policy Research Unit, SPRU, was concerned with policy not politics. I was fortunate to find the right person to run it, Christopher Freeman, who became a good friend. I established SPRU in 1966 before I became Vice-Chancellor. Its primary aim was to contribute through its researches to the advancement of knowledge of the highly complex social process of research, invention, development, innovation and the diffusion of innovation and thereby to a deeper understanding of policy for science and technology.

From this it is clear that the unit was problem-orientated rather than discipline-oriented. Its very diverse research projects were funded from non-UGC sources. They included the Research Councils, foundations, government agencies and private endowments. Through my efforts we won the support of a very useful private benefactor, Reginald M. Phillips, whom I used to see about once a week in his home where we discussed every kind of subject, the most central the pattern of his life. A former building speculator in London, he used the word plan as often as the economists of that period were doing.

His great hobby was stamp collecting, and he built up a superb collection of British stamps which he presented to the nation. They now constitute the Phillips Collection, managed by the Post Office. That brought back Tony Benn into my life. I had seen something of him when he was President of the Union in Oxford in 1947. He had been Postmaster-General before becoming Minister of Technology, and he liked Reginald. Our threesome meetings were always interesting and pointed us towards SPRU. When Reginald and I were on our own there were some funny moments. I once referred to the outbreak of the Great War in 1914. He burst in (was it anxiously?) 'Are you sure that the War began in 1914?' Through his benefactions he deserved more honours than the CBE conferred upon him. I believe that he and Christopher Freeman met only once when the University conferred an honorary doctorate on him.

I had met most of the people who worked within or for SPRU, particularly Roy MacLeod, a real scholar – and a brilliant one – who edited *Social Studies of Science*, which was committed to serving the growing community of historians (he put them first), philosophers, sociologists, political scientists and economists contributing research to the study of science in its 'social dimension'.

I had been personally interested in this process myself before I arrived in Sussex. I took part in symposia at the OECD in Paris and had contacts with the Club of Rome, which soon found itself clashing with SPRU. I corresponded regularly with Maurice Goldsmith, editor of *Science and Public Policy*, journal of the Science Policy Foundation, which I believe that he founded. It had national correspondents in twenty-seven countries, including Argentina, Canada, Denmark, Hungary, India, Japan, Mexico, Switzerland and the United States. The Science Policy Foundation was avowedly left-wing, and in the first number of *Science and Public Policy*, published in 1974, quoted S. D. Bernal's book *The Science of Science*, published ten years before, 'The awareness of the proper use of science in society is not easy to reach, and it is harder still to get agreement even among scientists.'

I have described elsewhere in this chapter my links with Stephen Toulmin who I now think was wise not to join us in Sussex. I am very glad that Roy MacLeod did. I had myself met most of the people involved in science policy research and felt a participant from the start in the work of SPRU and not an observer. I recognised how valuable it was in Sussex teaching as well as in Sussex research, and I appreciate how important it was that my successor as Vice-Chancellor, Denys Wilkinson, gave as much support to SPRU as I had done and that it found a perfect administrative secretary, Jackie Fuller. Chris's deputy, Geoffrey Oldham, came from Canada but had been born in Bingley on the road from Keighley to Bradford. A Ten Year Review panel appointed by the university included Sir Brian Flowers, then Rector of Imperial College, who was a good friend of mine and of SPRU.

I was interested in encouraging within the University the formation of all science research units whatever their particular concern. I liked to call them units and not institutes, whatever their size, and I knew that some would succeed and establish themselves and some not. Above all else there had to be flexibility and adaptability. They could not draw on our UGC budget funds unless the UGC wanted to move a unit here for which it was already responsible and which was being supported by a Research Council.

My favourite unit on the 'science side' at the university, as I myself considered it, was the Nitrogen Fixation Unit headed by Joseph Chatt, a northerner born in 1914. From 1942 to 1946 Chatt had been deputy and then chief chemist at a firm in Widnes which will figure through its rugby league club in my Chapter 5, 'Abiding Historical Interests'.

I never called the Nitrogen Fixation Unit Nitfix. Others in Sussex and outside did. It had origins that I can relate directly to my personal history outside Sussex. The Agricultural Research Council at that time was headed by Gordon Cox, whom I had watched and admired as a spokesman for the sciences when we were both on the Senate at Leeds. It was his idea at the ARC in 1963 to move Chatt's Fixation Unit from Queen Mary's College, London, to the University of Sussex. We were ready to give it an enthusiastic welcome and what it most needed, space. The unit arrived in Sussex in 1964.

There were links with my personal history. Chatt's deputy director in the Unit, John Postgate, was a brother of Richmond Postgate whom I knew through adult education and the BBC, where for a time he was Head of School Broadcasting, and who was to work with me in the creation of the Open University. Without any such links, I would, however, have given the unit my own enthusiastic backing. I knew how important it was – and urgent – to discover the chemistry and biochemistry of nitrogen fixation and was delighted when what I immediately thought of as *our* Nitrogen Fixation Unit was quickly judged to have the best laboratory of its kind in the world. It was to survive Chatt's retirement and to be directed next by John Postgate.

I end this chapter, which is bound to be selective, with the twenty-seven-page McKinsey Report, *Strengthening Participative Management*, dated September 1967, which was lying on my desk when I became Vice-Chancellor. In 2013 it is now a largely forgotten document, but its recommendations, which had been discussed at length with individuals and groups, changed the way in which the university worked, and without focusing in it on the relationship between the arts and the sciences, which were now organisationally separated. Arts and Social Studies were under the care of Barry Supple and the Sciences under the care of Colin Eaborn. They worked closely with me, but I had no part to play in the faculty appointments that they made or in their relations with the separate schools of study within their domain. These increasingly went their own way with elected Deans. I had a small team to work with me and for me.

John Fulton had commissioned the McKinsey Report in the late winter of 1966/67 at no cost to the University. It was the first report on a university made by McKinsey & Company, Management Consultants, who were later in my life to become major consultants to the BBC. I knew and liked their Chairman in 1967, Roger Morrison, who played no part in the discussions leading up to the finalisation of the report. Quite tangentially I add that Morrison lived in a London house where Bram Stoker, author of *Dracula*, had once lived.

McKinsey's approach to the companies who paid for their services was familiar to me in 1967. They wanted to be sure that their chief executives would like their recommendations and that they would welcome relief from duties that could be taken over by other people and, above all, freedom from a round of committees. I certainly felt that there were far too many committees at Sussex in 1967, and when

I turned to a long section headed 'Providing Support for the Vice-Chancellor', I felt that was what as Pro-Vice-Chancellor I had always offered to John Fulton, and what I knew Michael Thompson, a physicist, whom I had chosen as my Pro-Vice-Chancellor, would always offer me.

I also agreed with the McKinsey recommendation that 'a small effective management team should operate under the Vice-Chancellor to handle the many minor day-to-day issues and provide direction and a centralising influence to the University'. I was amused to read on the next page of the report, however, that the assignment of responsibilities should 'ensure' that 'many matters requiring immediate attention' could be handled 'even if the Vice-Chancellor is away'. John Fulton was so often away between 1965 and 1967, tied up with important outside responsibilities of national importance – the BBC and the constitution of the Civil Service – that the main implication for me of my becoming Vice-Chancellor was that I was now relieved of reporting to him, when from time to time he returned briefly to the University, on many matters about which he knew nothing.

The sixth section of the report, 'Implementing the Changes', suggested that general discussion on it should be completed by November 1967 and that the target date for implementing the McKinsey proposals should be January 1968. By then I would well and truly be Vice-Chancellor. Nonetheless, when I read the report I knew at once that, despite all the interviews and discussions that had taken place, and the approval of the Senate and the Council, dislike of the report in some sections of the University would be strong and sustained. There would be vociferously expressed dislike both of the content and of the language of the report. In some university circles the very word management itself was suspect.

It was not suspect, of course, with the Registrar, Geoffrey Lockwood, who had worked closely with Dick Finn of McKinsey on the preparation of the report. A few years later, however, he became a critic of it and in 1973 produced a report on the management of the University by a project team which he directed jointly with John

Fielden. The report was published by the Sussex University Press, a recently founded institution. It had the support of the University Grants Committee. The project team had ten members, two of them full-time, Fielden, who was to go on to become a consultant with Peat, Marwick, Mitchell and Co., and Robert Nind on leave from his duties as Secretary of Science at the University. The report created more interest outside the University than inside it.

Chapter 4

John Reith, Recalled, Reassessed

There were eight portraits of former BBC Director-Generals on view at a 'Faces and Folklore Exhibition' shown when Mark Thompson was Director-General between 2004 and 2012. I knew personally all eight of them, some of them extremely well, particularly the first and most famous of them, John Charles Walsham Reith, born in 1889, knighted in 1927 and created first Baron Reith of Stonehaven, a small town by the sea near Aberdeen, in 1940. In 1922, the year after I was born, he became Managing Director of the newly founded British Broadcasting Company, and it was largely through his imagination and determination but not entirely to his comfort that in 1927 the company was converted into the British Broadcasting Corporation by Royal Charter. It now had Governors not Directors. It did not need to change its initials.

When in 1987 the newly appointed eleventh Director-General, Sir Michael Checkland, walked into a crowded press conference in the Council Chamber of Broadcasting House, and it was pointed out to him that he was not a programme-maker Checkland turned his chair round and, looking up to the large portrait of Reith in the Council Chamber, he answered, simply and very much to the point, 'Neither was he.' After that no member of the press queried Checkland about his own credentials.

Reith's outstanding contribution to the establishment, independence of purpose and ethos of the BBC was known to everyone inside the Council Chamber that day and to most of those who were interested in broadcasting history outside it. Yet, as a person, Reith was a complex and contradictory character, often troubled and always arrogant. That was already known when he retired from the BBC and departed from Broadcasting House in 1938. There were no cameras to record the event at the time, but what was said or written about him then had the same tone as obituaries. Indeed, I consider them to be quasi-obituaries and I like to compare them with the real obituaries which were written after his death in 1971. There had been many twists and turns in Reith's fortunes and in those of the BBC in the years between 1938 and 1971.

When Checkland appeared at his press conference in 1987 he did not know that there was a genuine surprise in store for him. He was to learn that he was not only to gaze at Reith's portrait in the BBC's Council Chamber but to be called upon to write a foreword to a book written by Reith's daughter Marista, *My Father: Reith of the BBC*, which was published in 2006. It painted a completely different portrait of Reith from that hanging in Broadcasting House. Marista's intention was to reveal Reith as a father, husband and family man. She has much of interest to say, but she also reveals much of herself as a Reith daughter and as a sister to Reith's son. She had once told me at a memorial gathering in Caversham, where the written archives of the BBC are kept, that I was wasting my time writing about Reith and indeed about broadcasting.

So, too, did most professors of history and politics who thought I should have been writing about the Victorians instead. A notable exception was a future Gladstone Professor of Politics at All Souls College, Vernon Bogdanor, when he was still a Fellow of Brasenose College under a Warden, Lord Windlesham, who had himself been deeply involved in broadcasting. I should have mentioned him in *Special Relationships*. He knew how important the history of broadcasting is and that it is at its best when broadcasting institutions are viewed comparatively within and between countries.

To get my own writing record straight I must add that I did not stop writing about the Victorians while I was writing the history of the BBC. I have always liked to be writing more than one book at a time. I am doing so now. Academics had warned me that I would stop writing about the Victorians or indeed any books about history at all when I became Vice-Chancellor of Sussex. One was the Vice-Chancellor of Birmingham University, a university I knew well in a city that I knew even better. Robert Aitken, then the Vice-Chancellor of Birmingham University, admitted later to my wife that he had been completely wrong. I was proud when my deputy Vice-Chancellor and Acting Vice-Chancellor when I left Sussex in 1976, Michael Thompson, became Vice-Chancellor of Birmingham, via the Vice-Chancellorship of East Anglia, in 1987.

I got to know John Reith well while I was writing the first of what I originally contemplated as three volumes on the history of broadcasting in the United Kingdom. In 1958 I had accepted an invitation to write the history from the then Director-General of the BBC, Sir Ian Jacob, writing on behalf of the Governors. I knew full well from the start that it would be absolutely essential to have the support and cooperation of Reith to write the first volume. There was what might have been an intractable problem in the way. Reith almost despised Jacob and, indeed, the other leading figures in the BBC of 1958. I decided that the wisest course to follow was to write to Reith directly and tell him of the nature of my assignment.

I do not now have a copy of the letter that I sent to him, but in it I included an invitation to him to have lunch with me at my London club, the Oxford and Cambridge, in London's Pall Mall. Reith's own favourite club, the prestigious Athenaeum, was at the other end. I do *not* have a copy of his reply telling me that he would accept. I had met Reith only once before when he came to Worcester College, where I was then a Fellow and Tutor, to see his only son Christopher. Born in 1928, Christopher had been sent to Eton and was now reading agriculture and estate management in Oxford. I was Christopher's 'moral tutor' and I liked him. I never once talked to him about religion, as Reith doubtless thought that I would have been bound to do.

When in 1929 Reith interviewed the man who became the first editor of a journal devised by him, *The Listener*, Richard S. Lambert, the first question that he asked him and which took Lambert completely by surprise was 'Do you accept the fundamental teachings of Jesus Christ?' Reith had founded *The Listener* in face of vocal opposition from Fleet Street. Instead of embarking on an open argument with the Newspaper Proprietors' Association or receiving a deputation from them in his office Reith chose shrewdly to go round on his own to talk to them at their NPA office.

With twelve of its members on one side of the table and he alone on the other, he appears to have convinced them that in creating *The Listener* he was reconciling print and sound. He never consulted Lambert about what he was doing, and in a letter to me he suggested that some of his own Governors were not convinced that the BBC needed *The Listener*. Doubtless Lambert would have been amused to learn that after driving back to Savoy Hill with Lord Riddell, the NPA Chairman, whom he knew and liked, Reith wrote in his diary 'But, of course, it is the Lord helping me'.

There was more in it than that. Riddell had supported Reith when he founded the *Radio Times* in 1923. He saw the possibilities of broadcasting. The *Radio Times* has now celebrated its ninetieth birthday, and I include in *Loose Ends and Extras* several examples of its covers decade by decade as I do of cartoons of Reith. In 1981 I wrote an introduction to *The Art of Radio Times*, compiled by David Driver, art editor from 1964 to 1978, in which I claimed that the pages of *Radio Times* displayed (the right word) more of the folklore of broadcasting and the rhythms of the broadcasting year than it is possible to learn from any other single source. I praised the quality of its illustrations and the group of men, among them Edward Ardizzone, Peter Brookes and Ralph Steadman, who were responsible for coloured covers which were in themselves an attraction for readers.

When the BBC changed from company to corporation in 1927 the strikingly illustrated Christmas number sold a million copies. It cost sixpence. All other numbers, including what were called special numbers, cost two pence, as great an attraction as the illustrations. The Christmas numbers of the 1930s are interesting to compare as are the many special number covers of the 1930s, like a Fireside number,

Above: Ned Sherrin, from whose radio programme *Loose Ends* my book gets its title, with his friend and collaborator Caryl Brahms. Older than he was and with a long life of her own, they had what Ned called a constructive relationship.

Right: *Reader's Digest* played an important part in my writing and editorial activity, and I am sad that it is no longer to be published. Among these revealing covers I particularly like those for *Dr Who*, Nigella Lawson and the Queen's Diamond Jubilee. I used the large room in the New York Public Library endowed by the founders of *Reader's Digest* for much of my research there.

ASA BRIGGS

Daniel Snowman meets the co-founder of the University of Sussex and doyen of Victorian history.

THOUGHT, WORK AND PROGRESS: the key words of mid-Victorian England according to Asa Briggs. And they might stand as the personal motto of Lord Briggs of Lewes, a man whose monumental productivity as scholar, author and doer of good public works would have won him the plaudits of a Prince Albert or a Gladstone. But if the burghers of Leeds or Lewes ever decide to erect a statue of Asa Briggs, I hope they don't make it look too earnest, for he is the most engaging of men, utterly without pretension. 'I suppose I am a bit of a Victorian,' he acknowledges, but with an almost schoolboyish grin which instantly offsets any suggestion of stuffiness.

The author of *The Age of Improvement* was born in Keighley in 1921 and rose through sheer ability, and an unquenchable thirst for hard work, to become Professor of History at Leeds, co-founder and Vice-Chancellor of the University of Sussex, Provost of Worcester College, Oxford, Chancellor of the Open University, Chairman or President of a score of learned and historical societies and author of countless articles and books great and small. You can read Briggs on Victorian cities, people and things, on steam and transportation, public health and education, science and technology, music and literature, food and drink, sport and public entertainment, print and publishing, Chartism and the Channel Islands and, in five mighty tomes, on the history of British broadcasting. Chronologically he ranges from prehistory (in the opening chapter of his *Social History of England*) to the present and future (in *Fins de Siècle*), while his core writings about Victorian England are peppered with comparative material from or about Sydney and Melbourne, New York and Chicago, Dublin, Lyons, Tokyo and Berlin.

Samuel Smiles, apostle of self-help, would have approved. Grandfather Briggs, an engineer (like Asa's father), heard Smiles's lecture and told his grandson about them years later. 'My grandfather got me interested in

history,' Briggs recalls. 'He took me to every abbey and castle and small town in Yorkshire when I was a boy.' It was through his grandfather, too, that Asa developed a lifelong interest in science and technology. His mother's family farmed land in nearby Oxenhope where the cashier in the mill was a Mr Butterfield – whose son Herbert was also to become one of England's best-known historians.

A scholarship to Keighley Grammar School led Briggs, under the influence of a forceful and encouraging headmaster, to Sidney Sussex College, Cambridge. Here he famously obtained not only a Double First in History but also – concurrently (and in secret from his college) – a First in Economics as an external student at the LSE, which was evacuated to Cambridge during the war. Thus, Briggs was able to feast at the table of Postan and Saltmarsh, Oakeshott and Ernest Barker, Hayek, Laski and Eileen Power. He revelled in the *richesse*, devouring lectures, consuming books and pouring out weekly essays for both sets of masters on such diverse subjects as medieval and constitutional history, political philosophy and economic theory.

His versatility was soon to be stretched yet further. After a brief stint teaching at his old school, Briggs was called up into the Royal Corps of Signals where he learned Morse and was trained in fast interception. Then he received a call: he was to go on a cryptographic course – and thence to Bletchley where he spent three years as part of the top-secret team that broke the Enigma code.

While still at Bletchley, Briggs was wooed by both Oxford and Cambridge, finally accepting a Fellowship at Worcester College, Oxford, where he obtained a Readership and stayed for ten years. He was wooed by Churchill, too, who had asked Bill Deakin to recruit bright young historians (Alan Bullock was another) to help check the text of his forthcoming *History of the English-Speaking Peoples*. Apparently the curmudgeonly old aristocrat was graciously receptive

'Today's History' by my friend and collaborator Daniel Snowman, then working in the BBC, from an article in *History Today*, October 1996. Daniel had been teaching at Sussex University before he joined the BBC.

A view of the site, looking north, on which the science buildings of the University of Sussex were to be erected.

A gathering of the University Science Faculty at the opening of the Accelerator in 1970. It was a rare occasion when I addressed the Science Faculty entirely on their own.

Above: The Science Quad, University of Sussex, *c.* 1970.

Above: Basil Spence's University of Sussex Molecular Science Building, a main university centre for lecturers on all subjects from inside and outside the University.

Left: Inside the building, a science lecture is in progress.

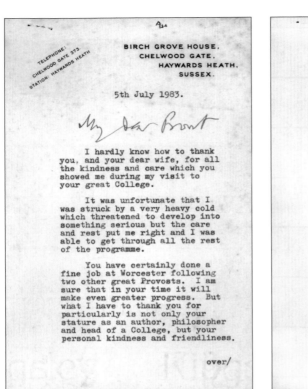

TELEPHONE:
CHELWOOD GATE 373
STATION: HAYWARDS HEATH

BIRCH GROVE HOUSE,
CHELWOOD GATE,
HAYWARDS HEATH,
SUSSEX.

5th July 1983.

My dear Provost

    I hardly know how to thank
you, and your dear wife, for all
the kindness and care which you
showed me during my visit to
your great College.

    It was unfortunate that I
was struck by a very heavy cold
which threatened to develop into
something serious but the care
and rest put me right and I was
able to get through all the rest
of the programme.

    You have certainly done a
fine job at Worcester following
two other great Provosts. I am
sure that in your time it will
make even greater progress. But
what I have to thank you for
particularly is not only your
stature as an author, philosopher
and head of a College, but your
personal kindness and friendliness.

over/

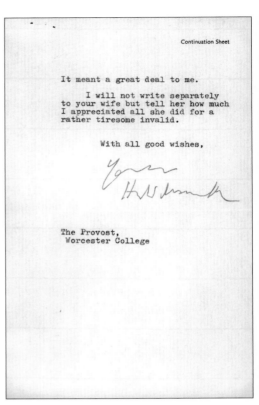

    It meant a great deal to me.

    I will not write separately
to your wife but tell her how much
I appreciated all she did for a
rather tiresome invalid.

       With all good wishes,

Yours
H.V. Macmillan

The Provost,
Worcester College

I invited Harold Macmillan as Chancellor of Oxford University to attend the celebratory dinner in Worcester College on the occasion of the 700th year since its foundation. I had known him well in Sussex when I was Vice-Chancellor of the University.

The bust of me sculpted by Kate Hall (now Lady Limerick), daughter of the owners of Breaky Bottom, our local vineyard. It was commissioned for the University of Sussex by Ben Whitaker, former Labour MP for Hampstead.

A SOP TO CERBERUS:
OR, THE DOGS' CHANCE.

[Uncensored talks by political leaders will be broadcast by the B.B.C. on nine consecutive Thursdays, beginning next month.]

Above: I did not know when I gave my talk 'Cerberus and the Sphinx' in Oxford in 1952 that I would find in writing *Loose Ends and Extras* a cartoon of John Reith, 'A Sop to Cerberus'. He was offering the three main British political parties, Labour (*left*), Conservative (*middle*) and Liberal (*right*) the opportunity of broadcasting uncensored political talks.

Above right: The most art nouveau cartoon of Reith. Would he have recognised himself?

Right: My favourite cartoon of Reith, by David Low. Reith was a perfect subject for cartoonists because of his height and the scar on his face.

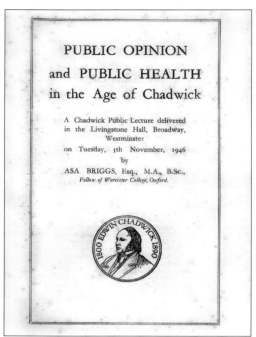

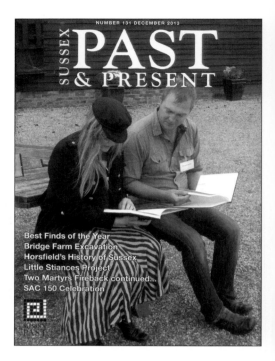

My first public lecture, published by the Chadwick Trust in 1946. I gave it first in Leicester, a city which has a diversity of associations for me. Edwin Chadwick is one of the most remarkable figures in nineteenth-century history. Born in 1800 he lived on until 1890.

Past & Present is the title of a book by Thomas Carlyle and of a notable history journal which deals with the chronological threesome – ancient, medieval, modern. Completing another threesome, *Past & Present* is also the name of the journal of the Sussex Archaeological Society.

My sporting life has been long and I remember well the great four-minute mile run by Roger Bannister when I was a young Fellow at Worcester. He and his wife Moyra are close family friends. We were delighted when Roger became Master of Pembroke in 1983 when I was Provost of Worcester.

Early Marks & Spencer bazaars. M&S described themselves as 'the originators of penny bazaars. Admission free.' In 1890 there were twenty-three penny bazaars in market halls, including in Rotherham, Sheffield, Scarborough, Southport, Warrington and Wolverhampton.

Above and left: The exterior and interior of a Victoria Wine store, one of the world's first chains of local wine shops. No two shops were quite the same.

Above right and right: Sketches taken from *Pictorial World* of the Victoria Wine Company's premises in Osborne Street, East London, in 1880.

Ground Floor

Examining Bottles

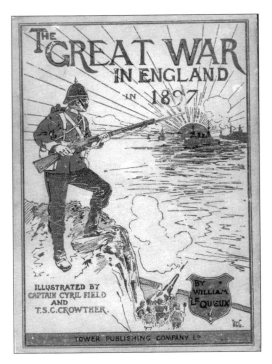

A 'Great War' had been anticipated long before the Great War of 1914–18 began. William Le Queux, the author, had no intimations of what the all too real and protracted Great War would be like.

One result of commemorating the Great War is the rediscovery of local links. In 2014 the Brighton Pavilion Trustees are honouring Vere Fane Bennett-Stanford, who was heir to Preston Manor, long part of the Pavilion complex, including in my years at the University of Sussex.

224 AULT   La plage vue des falaises

The last point on my trip to the Somme in 2013, where thanks to my son Daniel and daughter-in-law Anabel I was able to reach the village of Ault on the Channel coast. I had stayed there twice before the Second World War, the first time in 1934. For me this journey was one of rediscovery.

Left: The most famous episode from the *Blackadder* series, which first began in 1983, was the last one, shown in 1989, when Rowan Atkinson and Tony Robinson were at war in the trenches. It was a gripping programme, moving too, which was described by the Education Secretary Michael Gove as the kind of programme that should not figure in school commemorations of the Great War. Robinson fought back.

The Story of the Great Science Fiction
"Family" of the 30's
That Produced Today's Top SF
Writers and Editors

THE FUTURIANS

by Damon Knight

ASIMOV - BLISH - KORNBLUTH -
MERRIL - POHL - SHAW -
WOLLHEIM - AND MORE!

Sonny Ramphal, Secretary-General of the Commonwealth 1978–90, asked me to chair a committee which produced the blueprint for the Commonwealth of Learning. When it recently celebrated its twenty-eighth anniversary I was delighted to send a congratulatory message.

My well-rooted interest in science fiction has made me keenly interested in its history as a genre. Damon Knight's book, an insider account, is indispensable. Asimov is the best-known of his 'Futurians', a very different group from the Futurologists, many of whom I knew well.

With my dear friend K. K. Wong (*left*), who came from Hong Kong to see us at Tyninghame House (*right*).

饒宗頤文化館於二〇一二年六月二十二日開幕，其得以建成，實有賴特區政府對文物保護、活化以及對文化傳承和交流的重視，更是香港開埠以來首次大規模地對中華文化的發揚和傳承提供支持。從場地的篩選以至改造費用的資助，都實質上體現了對中華文化傳承的重視，更具體地宣揚了饒宗頤教授在學術和藝術上的成就，文化館的落成啟用見證了饒公作為當代中華文化的標誌。筆者有幸參與此項別具意義的工作，可以更近距離地聆教於饒公，故賦一詩以紀其盛，並附其英譯詩文。

文藝雙尊攜饒學
化俗紅牆聞鐸音
傳宗翠宇業千載
承澤南山濟眾心
荔熟夏林蔭學圃
灣深旭日照鳴禽
創圍啟動憑睿志
新猷建館紋古今

"Professor Jao, the light of culture and art,
Nurtures the young, with his purity of heart;
Within the red brick walls, lasting for thousand years,
Echoes resound in the mountain clear.
Blooming trees, twittering birds on the Lai Chee slope,
Cradle the morning sun, the guardian of hope.
With hearts united, let's create the new sanctuary,
Till the end of time and the enlightening of humanity."

Above: A poem I wrote while in China.

Left: Susan and I in China. We often visited K. K. Wong. He was as active a photographer as he was a poet.

In our son Daniel and daughter-in-law Anabel's garden on my ninetieth birthday, 7 May 2011, with our four children. From left to right, Katharine, Matthew, my wife and I, Judith and Daniel.

My wife and I in the garden at home, on a beautiful spring day in 2014. It was taken by my publisher, Michael Leventhal.

a Children's Hour number, an Outside Broadcasts number, a Woman's number and a Humour number, the last of them used on the dust cover of Driver's *Art of the Radio Times*. One of my own favourite covers is a black and white number of 1933 which features a forthcoming broadcast of Shakespeare's *Macbeth*.

I have favourite cartoons of Reith too. He was a tempting target even for indifferent cartoonists. His appearance was easily caricatured: his sheer physical presence, beetling eyebrows and the scar along his face naturally attracted attention. His activities, opinions, prejudices and achievements always demanded notice. My favourite cartoon was Low's which appeared in a supplement to the *New Statesman* in November 1938. That was the year when Reith left the BBC. I also liked Gilbert Frankau's in *The Strand* of March 1931. Frankau, who confessed that he was a little amazed that Reith was five years younger than he was, considered him a leader in 'an age of almost universal flabbiness', 'a man of forthright competence, who both understands and means to carry on with his job'.

The publishing arrangements for the *Radio Times* were very different and far more complicated than those for *The Listener* which was the BBC's own property. Reith made a business deal with George Newnes Ltd which left control of the new *Radio Times*, 'a Bradshaw of Broadcasting', with Newnes. Its editor, Leonard Crocombe, an experienced journalist who had edited *Titbits*, was responsible for its contents. From the BBC he merely received programme details. Some newspaper proprietors had thought that the BBC should pay advertising rates for publishing them in their newspapers. In planning his first issue, Crocombe knew that such details could not stand on their own, and he commissioned Sir Ernest Rutherford to write an article on 'The Miracle of Broadcasting'. He also decided to ask Reith to write an editorial in each number and to incorporate in each number a 'Children's Corner', to be written by Rex Palmer, 'Uncle Rex' of *Children's Hour*.

The first issue sold more than a quarter of a million copies, and Crocombe was an astute enough journalist to realise from the start that he should introduce articles in the *Radio Times* by listeners whose attitudes to broadcasting and opinions about it were very different from those of Reith's ideal listener. In the very first number there was an article by a so-called critical listener, P. J., stating that,

> It seems to me that the BBC are mainly catering for 'listeners' who own expensive sets and pretend to appreciate and under-stand only highbrow music and education 'snob stuff'. Surely, like a theatre manager they must put out programmes which will appeal to the majority, and must remember that it is the latter who provide the main bulk of their income.

In 1926 Crocombe was succeeded by Walter Fuller, who gave way a year later to Eric Maschwitz, perhaps the greatest of the editors of *Radio Times*, who not only knew how to write articles and choose illustrators and illustrations but wrote songs, including 'A Nightingale Sang in Berkeley Square'. After six years as editor, which covered the BBC's move from Savoy Hill to Broadcasting House, Maschwitz was succeeded by Maurice Gorham, an Irishman born in 1902 and educated at Stoneyhurst College, Lancashire, who had been made art editor in 1928. He was promoted in 1933 to become general editor and remained in charge for eight years, seeing the departure of Reith in 1938 and the BBC's move into war a year later. In 1941 he was appointed Director of the BBC's North American Services and in 1944 returned to Europe to direct the BBC's Allied Expeditionary Forces Programme, which, when war ended, became the Light Programme. He had been with the *Radio Times* when for a strictly limited audience BBC television had begun in 1936 and in 1946 he became somewhat uneasily for a year head of the relaunched Television Service. He left the BBC after a busy twenty-one years in 1947. In 1952 he wrote a useful book *Broadcasting and Television Since 1900*.

Already by 1929 more than a million copies of *Radio Times* were being sold each week. Reith had seen more clearly than Newnes that its circulation was bound to rise each year as the numbers of listeners rose, but he looked beyond numbers. In *Broadcast Over Britain*, in which he explained his decision in October 1923 to start the *Radio Times*, he stated that while his primary object was that BBC programmes of all stations for the ensuing week should be clearly displayed in its pages, he wished at the same time to present to its readers his own distinctive vision of the future of the BBC. 'I think it will be admitted by all [it was not] that to have exploited so great a scientific invention for the purpose and pursuit of "entertainment" alone would have been a prostitution of its powers and an insult to the character and intelligence of the people.'

I agreed wholeheartedly with this sentiment whether or not it was put into Reithian language, not all of which I liked, and by my taking it for granted, indeed, sharing it with him, I found it easy to cooperate with him when I was writing *The Birth of Broadcasting*. It was one of the matters that I discussed with him when I met him at my invitation in 1958 to discuss the first volume of my *History of Broadcasting in the United Kingdom*. I had carefully read and thoroughly digested *Broadcast Over Britain* before we met. I appreciated that it was a personal *cri de coeur* as well as a public manifesto and I was impressed that it had taken him, not used to writing, only seven weeks to write.

It was a momentous lunch. Determined to secure his support, I took care to give him as good a lunch as my club could provide. Fortunately it went off well. We conversed freely, mainly on his beliefs and working experiences during the 1920s before and after he wrote *Broadcast Over Britain*. After lunch there was a dramatic climax. As we went down the club steps, Reith, two steps below me, but still towering above me, called out to me in a loud Scots voice, 'Before you gave me this lunch I was not sure whether I would cooperate with you or not. Now I have decided that I will, but [a big but] if you had sent your letter to me on BBC paper I would have cast it into the flames.' Times had changed since 1923 when he was beginning to shape his new BBC. I had not then learnt to read, but I very soon did. The *Radio Times* soon became part of my regular reading.

By 1938, the year when he left the BBC, I was seventeen and not only was I reading a lot but writing a lot too. When I told him in my club about my assignment to write *The Birth of Broadcasting* and he said that he would cooperate with me he stuck to his word and cooperated unhesitatingly and wholeheartedly, inviting me to work in his London home in Lollard's Tower at the entrance to Lambeth Palace. I did so contentedly. On the desk before me he always left what seemed to be the relevant volume of his great diary, then unpublished, which was a unique source for my history.

As time went on he would leave a volume open at a page that I knew that he wanted me to read for his own reasons. It was usually quite irrelevant to *The Birth of Broadcasting* and might reveal the most intimate details of his life, including his passionate relationship with Charlie Bowser, a near neighbour in Glasgow, son of a Baptist minister, who was seven years younger than he was.

I have never written about this relationship, although it figures prominently, rather too prominently I believe, in Ian McIntyre's excellent life of Reith, *The Expense of Glory*, published in 1993, the best book about Reith yet written. Ian himself had his own relationship with the BBC, which he had joined in 1957, a year before I was invited by Jacob on behalf of the Governors to write my own history. He subsequently rose to be Controller of Radio 4, then of Radio 3, two BBC channels that could never have been contemplated during the 1920s. For Reith, who believed in a Home Service, never contemplated a Light Programme and never approved of a Third Programme, the very title of my fourth volume in my *History of Broadcasting in the United Kingdom: Competition* was anathema. He never abandoned his faith in the 'brute force of monopoly'. Until the advent of commercial television in 1955 most people in the BBC had faith in it too, although they would doubtless have cut out the adjective.

By the time that I had myself reached Bowser in reading Reith's diary my own cooperative relationship with Reith involved an elaborate routine which became a ritual. Before I went to work in Lambeth Palace he would send me inside an envelope a handwritten postcard bearing the words 'I will come next on . . . [date for me to fill in], I will arrive at . . . [time for me to fill in], I will have a good lunch.' I had to return my reply at once. As I went on with my book, using, of course, lots of other sources besides his diary, I would send him pages of *The Birth of Broadcasting* in draft to read and he would annotate them, very much to the point, sometimes asking me questions about what I had written. He never tried to force his own judgements on me.

I had no hesitation in dedicating my first volume to him. It appeared in 1962, the year when the University of Sussex took in its first students. By then Jacob, whom I did not once mention in it, had retired from his DG-ship and Hugh Carleton Greene had taken his place. Greene was tall enough to look Reith in the eye, and for a very brief spell the two men got on quite well. Reith even visited Broadcasting House again. But the relationship was soon over. For Greene, recalling it in an obituary which he wrote in 1972, Reith was 'an intensely subjective man who judged everything in the light of his own prejudices and convictions'.

This was a judgement shared by others which I had no reason to share. Reith had telephoned Greene – he loved the telephone – after seeing a *Radio Times* cover of which he disapproved. 'Do you not think Hugh', he asked, 'that the most important quality in life is dignity?' 'No, John,' Greene replied. 'There was a grunt at the other end of the phone and our conversation ended.' Thereafter Reith quite ruthlessly and totally broke off their relationship.

Reassessing what I wrote in *The Birth of Broadcasting* after an amazing fifty years in the life of the country, of the BBC and of myself, I turn back first to page 135, 'The Appointment of J. C. W. Reith', and to the seven pages that follow. Reith was only thirty-four years old. He had been born in the same year as R. H. Tawney, and in 1922 he knew as little about broadcasting as Tawney did. Reith had decided to apply for the post of General Manager of the BBC after having seen it advertised in a newspaper and he was required to send his application to Sir William Noble, a former Assistant Engineer-in-Chief of the Post Office who had joined the Marconi Company after the war.

And at this point Reith himself made a remarkable intervention of his own in determining what he took for granted was his 'destiny'. Having posted his letter to Noble in the Cavendish Club in Piccadilly he did what he said he should have done before and looked up Noble in *Who's Who*. There, having discovered that he was an Aberdonian, against club rules he retrieved his letter from the club post box and added this sentence to his application 'I am an Aberdonian and it is probable that you knew my family.'

Reith did not refer, of course, to the circumstance of his premature birth in Stonehaven, near Aberdeen which he was to choose as the placename of his title when he become first Baron Reith in 1940. His father and mother were on holiday there, and when it became clear that a birth was on its way his father had to go out in pouring rain and find a midwife. John was the Reiths' seventh child. His mother, Adah, was English, born in 1848: she had heard John Ruskin lecture and Dickens give his readings. She and George Reith, very much a Scot, married in 1870. They had six children before John, who was very much a Benjamin in the family. The age gaps between the Reith children were wide. Ernest was eighteen years older than John, who spent much of his childhood alone. It was a divided family. His relationship with his father, a commanding figure, was to be a strange one, and John later in life far too easily sentimentalised it. His mother called him Johnnie.

How in 1922 did Reith win the unanimous support of the makers of radio apparatus who were given the responsibility of running the BBC? In telling this story precise dates are essential. The BBC was formed on 18 October 1922 and registered on 13 December, but it was not immediately licensed by a slow-moving Post Office until 18 January 1923. The Chief Executive of the Post Office was Sir Evelyn Murray, whom Reith had not then met and with whom he was never to get on well.

It was on 13 December that Reith was summoned to Magnet House in Kingsway and appointed General Manager of the new BBC after the briefest of interviews. He was one of six applicants on a short list. Nothing official is known of the other five, but it has been claimed that one of them was a well-known national journalist. No one knew then, of course, that whoever became General Manager would be taking up a post that over time would become one of immense power. Reith shortened the length of time for it to do so.

On being told that he had been appointed Reith wrote in his diary 'I am profoundly thankful to God for His goodness in this matter. It is all His doing.' That was always Reith's manner of explaining the achievement of any object that he particularly desired. There were, however, human intermediaries in 1922 whom I clearly identified in *The Birth of Broadcasting*. There was also one other precise date in the chronology, the defeat of the coalition government of Conservatives and Liberals in the general election of November 1922, the results of which were announced on the 16th.

Reith had been working during the summer of 1922 for Sir William Bull, a Unionist politician who introduced him to many political leaders, including David Lloyd George and Austen Chamberlain. When they met, Lloyd George told Reith that he should become an MP himself. Reith did not go into detail about just what tasks he performed for Bull, although he noted in his autobiography *Into the Wind* (1949) that one of them was to distribute significant sums of money, some of it in cash.

It might have been called wasted money when the Unionists lost the general election of November 1922 and Andrew Bonar Law, a little-known Conservative politician, who had opposed the Coalition Conservatives, won a majority of seventy-seven over all other parties combined. It is interesting that even after the election Reith continued to work with Bull. Indeed, on 13 December, the day when he was interviewed in Magnet House for the General Managership of the BBC, he organised a London meeting at which those Unionist Conservative MPs who had retained their parliamentary seats decided on what would be their stance towards the Bonar Law government.

The most important of the Conservative Unionists and the one whom they considered their leader was Sir Austen Chamberlain. In the words of the most brilliant of the Conservative coalitionists, Lord Birkenhead, 'He had the almost complete certainty that the time would come when he would attain the title of Leader and Prime Minister.' For Garry Allighan, Reith's first biographer, he visualised a new alignment of political forces of the two great anti-socialist parties bound by the tie of fighting for the 'common cause of the economic and social system they equally shared against the common Socialist enemy'.

It did not happen like that in 1922. Bonar Law became Prime Minister, but he resigned almost at once on grounds of health and died in 1923. Stanley Baldwin then became Prime Minister in his place. Reith was to establish a special relationship with him. He visited 10 Downing Street for the first time just after Baldwin became Prime Minister, and although Baldwin lost the subsequent general election – as the Unionist supporters of a coalition had predicted that he would do – the minority Labour government, Britain's first Labour government led by Reith's fellow Scot Ramsay MacDonald, lasted only for a few months and Baldwin became Prime Minister again.

Austen Chamberlain, no longer thinking, if he ever did, of 'a common socialist enemy', was Baldwin's Foreign Secretary and concentrated on the affairs of Europe. For a very brief period his brother Neville was Postmaster-General. Between 1922 and 1924 Reith had to deal with five of them. Baldwin's Chancellor of the Exchequer was Winston Churchill.

It was during Baldwin's second premiership, in 1926, that the General Strike occurred – another first in British history. I have written a lot about it in many places, and in *Loose Ends* I will concentrate entirely on the role of Reith. In his diary on 23 April he noted that it was imminent. It was the last diary entry that he made for a fortnight, and when he resumed writing it he expressed regrets that he had had no time to write about the strike while it was on. His diary could have been much fuller and much more interesting.

The strike had lasted for only nine days, what Reith called nine 'most happy' days for him. His main task had been to ensure that the BBC provided regular news bulletins for a news-hungry public. The news had to be reliable as well as regular. He conceded that the first bulletins were 'pretty rotten', but believed that they improved particularly when he began to read some of them himself. (So did his deputy, Admiral Carpendale, on whom he was coming to depend totally.) On the ninth day Reith was reading the one o'clock bulletin when news came through that the TUC leaders had been to No. 10 to tell the Prime Minister that they were calling off the strike.

In the evening bulletin, which he again read, Reith introduced a note of drama into the news. For once he was acting like a theatre manager. 'In going to work tomorrow or the next day', he asked his listeners, 'could we not all go [ahead] united in a determination to . . . build up the walls of a more enduring city – the city revealed to the mystic eyes of William Blake.' As a climax Reith launched into a reading of Blake's *Jerusalem*. It was a foretaste of the last night of the Proms, and he actually brought in an orchestra to play it in the background. The bulletin ended with full orchestra and chorus singing the last verse.

The strike left the BBC more independent and more influential than before the general election of 1926. Reith and Baldwin shared the same outlook. If Churchill had had his way, the BBC would have been commandeered. As it was, Baldwin made Reith a member of the Strike Committee of the Cabinet. At meetings of this Committee Reith and Churchill took opposing views. This was one of the many occasions on which their views diverged totally. This may have been that the two of them were temperamentally similar, but that, if true, was not the source of their differences.

Six years after the General Strike the BBC moved from Savoy Hill to Broadcasting House. Reith described this as the end of an era. When he left his room in Savoy Hill he bade it an affectionate farewell. He did not like Broadcasting House. The 1931 BBC *Year Book* said that in moving to new headquarters there would be 'numerous and better proportioned studios, perfectly isolated from one another', but for various reasons it was not the studios but the entrance hall which created most public interest. Reith did not talk much to the architect G. Val Myer, who had designed the House not with Reith in mind but to meet the functional requirements of broadcasting staff. Yet Reith talked a lot to the BBC's Consulting Engineer, Marmaduke Tudsbery, who it was said was the only man who chose to call Reith Walsham.

In the entrance hall there were Latin inscriptions devised by Montague Rendall, a former headmaster of Winchester and one of Reith's Governors, who had had carved out the dedicatory words *Deo Omnipotenti*. Reith approved of them, but doubted whether the BBC would live up to them. Rendall had also devised the BBC's English motto 'Nation shall speak peace unto nation'. The world could certainly not live up to that. It was not the Latin inscriptions that most interested the public and the media in 1932 but Eric Gill's symbolic depiction of Prospero and Ariel, placed on the face of the building above its main doors. This was scarcely an expression of Reithian philosophy. When Reith was given an honorary Doctor of Laws degree at Manchester in 1933 his presenter compared him with Prospero. He was the chief of the magicians by whose agency 'this isle is full of noises, sounds, sweet airs which give delight and hurt not'.

The objections to Gill's sculpture had nothing to do with Shakespeare. Ariel's genitals were considered lewd by people who might never have entered Broadcasting House, and a question was asked about the sculpture in the House of Commons. A Labour MP thought that it was offensive to public morals and decency, and urged the Metropolitan Police to remove it. Rendall, called in by the Governors as arbiter, judged that there was no offence in it. That was it.

I described the move to Broadcasting House and all the reactions to it and ramifications of it in the second volume of *The History of Broadcasting in the United Kingdom*. It was called *The Golden Age of Wireless, 1927–1939* and I dedicated it, knowing that Reith would approve of my dedication, to J. H. Whitley, Chairman of the Board of Governors from 1930 to 1935. I did not tell him that I was going to do so. I did tell him that I hoped that he would read my drafts as carefully as he had read the drafts of my *Birth of Broadcasting*. It very soon became clear to me that he was displeased with the draft text of *The Golden Age*.

Having studied the draft text of its first three chapters he commented to me that it seemed to him that 'someone may have said to you that there was too much of me in the first volume and please to rectify this in the second'. No one had. Nor had any of my reviewers. Now using 'please' himself, he went on 'Now please do not be angry with me.' He was less bothered about the space that 'some people and things get' than the inference which readers might draw that he had 'withdrawn in the cloud' and had not done 'anything like as much work for the BBC in the twelve years of the Corporation as in the four years of the Company'.

He obviously felt strongly about this. 'In fact I did fully as much and I think a good deal more, because I had an extremely troublesome Board [he added in ink to a typed letter] owing to the combination of Clarendon and Mrs. Snowden.' In making comments on the draft of *The Birth of Broadcasting* he had never written to me quite in this tone, and he certainly would never have added his next very general sentence of judgement, 'Also all sorts of things that I know to have been exceedingly important have not been alluded to at all, or they have only very casually.' The only specific example he gave was the start of *The Listener*. 'I think that this was one of the best things I did for the BBC.' I agree! He added a final question 'Was the Diary not so much good to you from 1927 as before that?' It was! I resented his sting in the tail. 'Or were you not able to give it so much time?'

The Golden Age got some very good reviews but, as in the case of all my later volumes, some reviewers were most anxious to say what they themselves thought about the BBC rather than deal seriously with my text. In one extraordinary review by Malcolm Muggeridge he felt that I had not dealt in depth with Reith. It was a clever-clever review which he called 'The Age of Reith'. He wanted to sound witty:

> Professor Briggs is no Gibbon, nor even a Trevor Roper. He writes like a man diligently plodding his way across a vast muddy plain ... facts and names abound; programmes, listeners, internal organisation, controversies over political and religious broadcasting, finance, personnel – nothing is left out ... As a result we have a usable work of reference which will rightfully take its place in all newspaper libraries between *Jane's Fighting Ships* and *Debrett*. In honesty, I must add that I cannot see how the job could have been tackled otherwise.

Before Reith died in 1972, the BBC's fiftieth anniversary year, I had taken part in 1969, when Reith was eighty, in a twenty-minute programme about him. Extracts from various recordings of him were included, among them his *Face to Face* interview with John Freeman. So were extracts from a BBC Library statement by Mary Agnes Hamilton who had been close to Reith when she had been a BBC Governor from 1933 to 1937. I was specially recorded in 1969 for the programme.

I did not like to be called by the narrator 'the BBC's official historian', for I knew that Reith would never have cooperated with me in 1958 if I had been. As it was, I had the first word in 1969. I was conscious, I said, of the 'tremendous presence of Reith, both physical and moral'. He was a man 'quite out of the ordinary whose ways of thinking and feeling are quite distinctive'. Quite rightly, Mary Agnes Hamilton was given the last word. She posed three questions, adding after them as an answer the two decisive words 'of course':

> Wasn't it he who gave it [the BBC] its shape as a public service corporation? Who secured its political independence? Who sought for and maintained its total freedom from the commercial pressures that distort broadcasting in other countries and established for it a reputation for efficiency and incorruptibility that are their envy?

After the 'of course' came the perfect sentence to end this programme. 'His fame is safe for the history books.'

I do not know what Reith thought of this programme or indeed whether he heard it. Early in 1968 his heart had begun to trouble him, and at the end of February he was admitted to the King Edward VII Hospital for Officers and kept there for nineteen days before being moved to the National Heart Hospital. There he spent six weeks and had a pacemaker fitted. He was allowed home at the beginning of April, convalescing in the gardens of Lambeth Palace and briefly in the Royal Crescent Hotel in Brighton. I did not know at the time or later that he was there. When the hotel was full at weekends, he grumbled, many 'ghastly people' were visitors, 'people who did not know how to hold their knives and forks properly'.

How did this Reith relate to the Reith of the eightieth birthday programme, a fourth question to add to Mary Agnes Hamilton's three? Yet there was worse to come for an aged-looking Reith. His hearing was going and he began to forget the names of people he knew well. Nevertheless, he was able to write in a diary that was now full of gaps that it would be wonderful if 'God had some tremendous work for me to do even at 80'. Soon afterwards he was proud to be made a Knight of the Thistle, the highest honour for a Scot to receive, to be installed in St Giles, and at the dinner in Holyrood Palace that followed to sit next to the Queen on her left. He had twice been her Lord High Commissioner to the Church of Scotland, living in Holyrood, and in 1970 she offered him a grace and favour residence in Edinburgh.

During the first decade of its life he had shaped the BBC, fully committed and deeply involved. During the 1930s, when the BBC was bigger and more complex, constitutionally different through his own proposals, he did not feel he was fully stretched, one of his favourite expressions. Other people were responsible for its operations. Yet, in *Into the Wind*, he stated in the plainest language '[it was] foolish of course to have left the BBC: stupendous folly to have left one of the most responsible and rewarding posts in all the world'.

In my view Reith, a man of contradictions, would have made a disastrous Director-General in wartime, particularly with Churchill as Prime Minister, and an even worse one in the years to follow. When Neville Chamberlain made him Minister of Information in 1939, press comment on his appointment was favourable. *The Times* wrote that the qualities needed in the Minister were grip and drive and that Reith had both but – and there are almost always buts in judgements on the post-BBC Reith – it concluded with the words 'The one doubt about him is whether his long enjoyment of an independent command may have rendered it difficult for him to collaborate in a team.'

That was not to be Reith's problem. He had always liked working with teams. When he was in the Army he preferred travelling with 'his men' to travelling with his fellow officers. When Neville Chamberlain appointed him head of Imperial Airways in 1938 he would have liked to have met its pilots and its crews first. He was appalled by the Imperial Airways headquarters in Buckingham Palace

Road and by the fact that it incorporated a railway station selling passenger tickets.

There was irony in his losing the post of Minister of Information when Chamberlain gave way as Prime Minister to Churchill. That was two days after Leo Amery on behalf of the Conservatives had called out to Chamberlain in the Commons, repeating Oliver Cromwell's words to the seventeenth-century Long Parliament, 'You have sat too long here for any good you may have been doing . . . For God's sake go.' The irony lay in the fact that in 1922 Reith, working with Bull, had distributed moneys to Conservative Coalitionists wishing to maintain a coalition led by Lloyd George, and that in 1940 he lost his post as Minister of Information when an exclusively Conservative government gave way to a coalition headed by Winston Churchill. There was irony for Churchill too. As a Coalitionist Conservative he had lost his seat at the general election of 1922.

Political memories in Britain are short and journalists seldom attempt to lengthen them. Reith's first biography, *Sir John Reith*, by no means the least interesting of his biographies, had appeared in 1938, written by a journalist, Garry Allighan, who called it an unusual one. Not only was it a biography of a living man but it was not as laudatory as 'literary tradition' demanded a biography should be. Lord Gainford, first Chairman of the Board of Directors of the British Broadcasting Company, wrote in the most sober of language an undated foreword to Allighan's book. Allighan, however, had literary pretensions of a romantic kind. His first sentence read 'No romance is more fascinating than that which is woven from the realities of life, of clashing wills and heroic achievements, of blood and tears, of living and dying.'

Allighan gives many instances of all these, bringing back to life many people who barely figured in Reith's own writings and describing many incidents which have passed out of remembered history. Ending his book in the year 1935 he discussed television, a subject which did not interest Reith in the least. Indeed, when he was looking at the text of the second volume of my *History of Broadcasting in the United Kingdom*, Reith handed the ninety-five pages on the beginning of the BBC television service to read to Sir Harold Bishop, Deputy Chief Engineer. He did not bother with them himself.

Television was the main concern of the journalist and radio critic Sydney Moseley who backed John Logie Baird. 'It was not the sweetest pill for the BBC chief to swallow', remarked Allighan, when the then Postmaster-General, Sir Kingsley Wood, a politician whom Reith abhorred whatever post he held, set up a committee to investigate the introduction of television in Britain and the BBC was authorised (in other words instructed) to start it. In 1933 Moseley had produced the kind of book on broadcasting that Reith most disliked, *Who's Who in Broadcasting*, and it must not have pleased Reith when, two years later, he published *Broadcasting in My Time*. It would have seemed a travesty to Reith. In 1960 Moseley was to bring out his *Private Diaries*. How in the world could they compare with Reith's that had not yet been published?

Allighan divided his *Sir John Reith* into four parts, and 'Machine and Master Mechanic', the fourth part, is the only part of his biography where he ceases to be laudatory about Reith. He begins one section of it with the observation that while Reith would be 'the first to denounce the dictatorial, undemocratic methods' of Italian fascists, his own critics were denouncing his BBC management policies as in need of thorough change. Harold Laski, a perceptive judge of Reith, was more specific. He justifiably detected a Mussolini within him. When, in November 1935, Reith entertained Marconi he told him that he had always admired Mussolini immensely.

I found – and find - the first part of Allighan's biography, 'The Pre-BBC Period', in which he dealt with Marconi, the most interesting. 'It is impossible to place a finger in the leaves of the Book of Time and say "Here began radio",' others, like Ambrose Fleming, inventor of the thermionic valve in 1904, had an important part to play in the story. Very early in the history of the BBC, in December 1922, before Reith as its General Manager had quite realised what broadcasting was, he was introduced to the Radio Society of Great Britain and decided to attend its next meeting to find out more about broadcasting. He wrote immediately afterwards that he had felt like Daniel in the den of lions – and said so. It was made clear to him there that he was an interloper, not a pioneer – 'a horrid embarrassment'.

The Radio Society of Great Britain had been founded in 1913, and its story had been interrupted by the Great War but not ended by it. It was pure speculation on Allighan's part to say that as young John Reith read of its wartime activities in his home in Scotland his interest in radio was 'quickened', but it is a fact that in wartime Britain, when the state called in all personal radio apparatus and dismantled home aerials, Captain Donnisthorne, a radio experimenter since 1910, was drafted by the War Office into its radio service. In 1917 he was brought back from France to England to train drafted servicemen in the use of Captain Round's wireless valves which derived from those of Ambrose Fleming.

One of the servicemen he trained was Noel Ashridge, future Chief Engineer of the BBC after Peter Eckersley. In the course of his duties Donnisthorne constructed a complicated transmitting apparatus to relieve the monotony of simply sending out Morse and of listening to it, by radio telegraphy. He experimented with radio telephony and broadcast gramophone record concerts. These were heard by troops in Worcester, in Malvern, home of Second World War radar, and in Droitwich, where in 1924 the BBC was to install a great transmitter that made possible the broadcasting of alternative programmes. This was to be the chosen scene of Reith's departure from the BBC in 1938.

When an announcement was made in July 1938 by Ronald Norman, Chairman of the BBC's Board of Governors, that Reith was leaving, this generated a mass of pseudo-obituaries. The news, he stated, had come as a 'great shock' to the Corporation itself. 'Broadcasting owed much to his dominant personality.' This was an understatement, as Norman knew, and there was a hidden story behind it:

> Nothing but a sense of urgent national importance would have taken him [Reith] away, and he would never have consented to leave his great work here except from the highest motives of public duty.

The country, he implied, was calling him to great things. Reith wished for and expected quite different great things. His diary for the spring of 1938 skips between Imperial Airways, first mentioned on 9 March, and the War Office.

Knowing this, we know too that Norman was in a position to write a real obituary. 'In other hands [than Reith's] broadcasting might so easily have been little more than a vehicle for the provision of popular entertainment.' Under his guidance it became 'one of the most valuable influences on the life of the country'. His 'width of vision embraced not only the passing desires but the permanent needs of Society [capital S] as a whole'. Reith gave to British broadcasting that character and those qualities which 'we now take for granted'. And then Norman remembered the particular BBC audience that he was addressing. 'Only a very unusual man, I know you will agree, could have built up from the beginning so unusual and vast an enterprise.'

Norman, successor to Reith's most congenial and helpful Chairman of Governors, J. H. Whitley, concluded his announcement with the words 'Every listener will, I know, wish him good fortune and success in his new and arduous post,' but nowhere 'will he have more sincere well-wishers than those he leaves behind on the Board and staff of the BBC. To him we all say fare well.'

Norman was then six months over his five-year term of office, and for a time Reith had thought that he might succeed him. So had some of the other Governors, who felt that Reith should only be seconded to Imperial Airways, the public job Neville Chamberlain, the Prime Minister, was asking him to take over. To Reith's disgust it was Kingsley Wood, then Secretary of State for Air, who made the announcement in the House of Commons that he was going to be appointed Chairman of Imperial Airways.

After Reith had taken the chair for the last time at the weekly meeting of the BBC's Control Board on 21 June 1938 he left Broadcasting House without ceremony, and with no photographers to show him leaving, took the lift down from his room with his wife Muriel, who shook the hand of the old lift man when they got out. He had no intention of going into Broadcasting House again. His break with the

BBC was to be final. Nevertheless, on the evening of leaving the Corporation he did what he was to call in *Into the Wind* a 'silly thing'. With three or four others he was driven to Daventry to close down for the night all the big oil engines that fed the Droitwich high-power transmitter. Those he had proudly inaugurated twelve years before with the then Postmaster-General. Now he simply signed the visitor's book 'J. C. W. Reith, late BBC'.

I must relate Reith's departure from the BBC, which was not to be as final as he then intended, to another crucial date in BBC history, the farewell to Admiral Charles Carpendale, Carps, who had joined Reith in July 1923 in the days of the Company and remained a loyal deputy to him until he retired, just before Reith left, in March 1938. In his summarised diary Reith wrote then that it was difficult to think of the BBC without him: 'I doubt if I can.' Very soon afterwards people were saying similar things about him. A fascinating element in the Carpendale story is that Reith frequently met Carpendale between his retirement and Reith's move to Imperial Airways. *The Times* in a leader saluted Reith's acceptance of the first full-time chairmanship of Imperial Airways while observing that the news of his appointment would come as a shock: it would take time for millions of listeners to accustom themselves to the change.

It was hardly too much to say that the BBC was Reith's creation. 'Had he yielded to "popular clamour" at the beginning it would have become the tame and monotonous purveyor of a rather base form of entertainment.' He could leave Broadcasting House in the knowledge that his pioneer work, now brought to maturity, had not to wait for the approval of posterity. At the age of forty-eight he was giving up what any man might be proud to call a life-work and turning pioneer again.

It was not only *The Times* that emphasised Reith's pioneering. The *News Chronicle*, then an influential newspaper, which Reith disliked as much as he did Beaverbrook's *Daily Express*, referred to his 'pioneer work' with the BBC. Its editor, Gerald Barry, was to play a big part in my own life. I saw a lot of him when I was a professor at Leeds University. Granada Television had endowed a Television Fellowship there, the first in the country. In the years leading up to the Festival of Britain in 1951, which Barry directed, I learned all of his plans. In style and outlook no two men could have been more different than him and Reith.

When I gave the third Mansbridge Memorial Lecture at Leeds in 1966 on 'The Communications Revolution', a term that I was one of the first, if not the first, to use, I quoted Barry not Reith. 'Twenty years from now' Barry wrote as an ex-editor, 'there will have been accomplished a technical revolution in both the printing and presentation of news comparable to the revolution of printing itself.' Barry thought more of news when he considered broadcasting than I do and I think Reith also.

The newspaper article on Reith that impressed me most at the time in the summer before I went up to Cambridge as an undergraduate appeared in the *Birmingham Mail*, 'Sir Ariel takes wings'. The leader writer called Reith's move more than a change of jobs. It would not escape the 'imaginative' that 'our new civil Air Pilot in Chief has won his wings in the uncharted ether'. Reith was not unimaginative, but he did not see his change of jobs in this way. He wanted a bigger and quite different job – Minister of Defence, Ambassador to the United States, Viceroy of India.

I did not read again a piece in *The Economist* about Reith's move in 1938 until after I had started *Loose Ends*. There was no imagery in it. 'Sir John Reith's resignation closes the first and critical chapter in the history of broadcasting.' Like Montagu Norman, the Governor of the Bank of England, who was outside the field of politics proper, he was one of the few men of outstanding personality in British public life. 'And around personality controversy always rages.' In 1937 the two controversial figures met. Montagu Norman invited the Reiths to join him on a cruise to the Caribbean and on through the Panama Canal. Muriel refused, saying that it was too long too be away from her two young children, and so John went on his own. It changed his life, for he spent a long time on board ship in the company of a young woman passenger, Helen Moir, and when they all got back to England he continued to see and flirt with Helen, against Muriel's objections.

He was following, he said euphemistically, 'a new policy of greater sociability'. He continued to follow it through the rest of his life.

In 1937 when Reith's BBC career was near to coming to a close, he decided to fulfil an ambition and write a book about the Great War. The more books that he had read the more it seemed to him, as he put it in *Into the Wind*, that during the war he had experienced what others had not and not experienced what others had. He used the opportunity of a BBC holiday to write a book and get it off his mind, and finished his first draft of about 80,000 words in a fortnight – an inspiration to me in writing *Loose Ends and Extras*. He then sent the manuscript of *Wearing Spurs* to six individuals, asking them to give him advice on its publication.

They did not recommend it. One of them was Ronald Norman, his last BBC Chairman, another the second-in-command of his old regiment. 'This is exactly what your enemies have been waiting for,' they said. 'Stay in the clouds, my dear friend.' And so he put his text away in a drawer until the 1960s and did not publish it until September 1966, five years before his death. His publisher, Sir Robert Lusty, had become a Governor of the BBC in 1961 and loved to tell anecdotes about Reith. He thought that *Wearing Spurs* would become a bestseller and mentioned it selling a million copies. It sold 5,000. When Lusty sent him a royalties cheque Reith asked him why he had left a nought off it.

The book was widely and favourably reviewed. Malcolm Muggeridge, who had entered Reith's life late, gave it a particularly favourable review in the *Observer*. 'It is not easy to put one's finger on just what gives its narrative its unique quality,' he wrote, 'I should say myself it is its truthfulness. People lie habitually about war as they do about sex and about money. War literature is a kind of power pornography.' Reith's fellow Scot Eric Linklater offered a simpler judgement. 'What a cracking good read', but he added his own imagery. 'His hundred-horsepower zeal must have been like a Rolls Royce engine condemned to drive a wheelbarrow.'

The truth was somewhat different or somewhat more complicated. Reith loved to see himself in a uniform – he was not, of course, alone in this – and after he returned from Gresham to Glasgow at the age of seventeen he joined the Glasgow University company of the Lanark-shire Rifle Volunteers and the next year when Glasgow acquired an Officer Training Corps he was one of the first three cadets to be made a sergeant, and he was also one of the first three to win his certificate which carried him straight to field rank without having to take any further examinations. He was given a gold star to place over his sergeant's stripes. He thought this magnificent. He could 'form a good opinion of himself' for the first time. He had achieved something in the world.

What happened next was not so satisfying. When war was declared in August 1914 the adjutant of the 5th Scottish Rifles, whom he called scarcely tactfully 'a little man', had apparently sent his mobilisation papers to an incomplete telegraphic address, and Reith complained to his commanding officer. There was then an anticlimax. His battalion was summoned not to France but to Falkirk as its war station. Ten days later, however, they were ordered south, eventually to one of the best remembered places in the folklore of the Great War, Armentières.

Reith had thus chalked up another two personal firsts. The 5th were the first Territorials to get to France, and he was the first Scottish Territorial to look at the trenches. There was as much gossip as folk-lore in Armentières. Sometimes one was converted into the other. Some gossip was true. Lord Roberts had died at St Omer. The King and the Prince of Wales actually did inspect the 5th Battalion. Reith was impressed by the inspection, but he considered that the King, with whom he shook hands, looked worried. He imagined him saying 'I can't find the words to say what I feel.'

This is not the place to recapitulate Reith's subsequent experiences in France except to say that by December Armentières was being heavily shelled and that it was by his own foolish behaviour that he continued to be in danger after he was transferred to the Sappers. He was wounded in a narrow trench and acquired his famous scar. It measured five inches by three. He was told at first that he would be in hospital back in Britain for months and that a silver plate might be fitted into his face. Yet the wound healed surprisingly quickly.

In the months after the General Strike of 1926 Reith went on a somewhat nostalgic holiday with his wife to see Great War sites, among them the house where he had been billeted in Armentières and a British military cemetery near Le Tréport, where Muriel's brother, killed in the war, was said to be buried. Summing up the whole trip he wrote in his diary, 'We found splendid trenches, three or four shells, tins of old bully beef and jam tins and barbed wire. It was most thrilling and M was quite overcome.' I am thrilled to read from his summarised diary that before going off on this trip he had left behind for Carpendale a twenty-seven-page memorandum headed 'Loose Ends'.

As my 'Extra' I add that when I was a schoolboy I stayed for two successive summers in a holiday villa not far from Le Tréport. I explain in more detail in my chapter on the Great War how I went back in 2013 on a somewhat nostalgic trip to the Somme which had been the scene of horrific battles with terrific loss of life. My son drove me there by car using the Channel Tunnel. I did not get as far as Cambrai where Jacques, the French schoolboy with whom I stayed, was a pupil at the *lycée*. It was the scene of a great battle beginning on 20 November 1917 when British Mark IV tanks, which had been devised by Lieutenant Colonel Ernest Swinton, penetrated the Hindenburg Line with a far smaller loss of life than in the trench warfare of the Somme.

The years between the General Strike and John and Muriel's visit to the Somme and his retirement from the BBC in 1938 were not without incident. The silliest but in some ways most serious trial that Reith confronted had come in 1935. It concerned 'the talking mongoose case', a slander action which involved Richard Lambert, the editor of *The Listener*, and Sir Cecil Levita, and which Reith failed to keep out of the law courts, although he did his best to do so. Coming before the King's Bench in November 1935 and lasting only three days, it had a dramatic ending. Lambert had employed the famous advocate Sir Patrick Hastings as his counsel, and the jury awarded him the huge sum of £7,500. The BBC Chairman, R. C. Norman, knew Levita slightly: he had served with him on the London County Council, and felt that the amount of money awarded to Lambert was grossly excessive. Reith, who knew Lambert well, felt so too and wrote in his diary that the jury's verdict had been 'quite amazing and monstrous', showing 'how rotten the jury system is'. He was on dangerous ground in making this generalisation. Norman, more circumspect, persuaded Baldwin, the Prime Minister, to set up a Special Board of Enquiry to look further into allegations made during the trial.

Its chairman was Sir Josiah Stamp, chairman of the London Midland and Scottish Railway, and his report, which criticised both Lambert and the BBC, recommended that the BBC should study civil service practice in dealing with staff matters. That was anathema to Reith, who had always resisted demands from some Governors and some BBC staff to do this. When Stamp's Report was published as a White Paper it was dismissed by supporters of change as a whitewashing exercise. Far more drastic action was needed. Lambert, highly critical of his employers, had exposed serious faults in BBC practices. Reith was greatly embarrassed to read all this at a point in his BBC career when he was getting tired of directing the Corporation. He even wrote in his diary on 19 March 1938 that he was getting bored with keeping it.

On 20 July 1938 he wrote in his diary after leaving the BBC 'I now enter my fiftieth year ... Last night my successor's name was announced on the wireless so, of course, the papers are full of it this morning and this vies with the King and Queen's visit to Paris for placard attention.' He had been annoyed with Norman for asking him on the phone two days before to let him have his resignation in writing 'just for tidiness sake'. He was suffering from lumbago and felt no enthusiasm for his successor, Frederick Ogilvie of Queen's College Belfast. He wrote to wish him well only at Carpendale's suggestion.

Towards the end of his life, when the Reiths had moved to a new home in Edinburgh, he had a calamitous fall in May 1971 which was to be his ultimate fall after many. Going out of his study he caught one foot on the other and crashed backwards, full length, breaking his thigh bone near the hip and severing all the ligaments in his knee. After hopeless hospital treatment he died in the Officers Nursing Home on 16 June. The announcement of his death in *The Times* stated unambiguously that on Reith's personal instruction the funeral would be private. It took place in the Thistle Chapel in St Giles. About twenty people were present.

Reith did not quite get his way. Four weeks later there was a service in Westminster Abbey, with lots of music, which began with un-accompanied singing by the BBC Chorus, followed by Sir Adrian Boult conducting the BBC Symphony Orchestra in music by Elgar and Vaughan Williams, and ended with the whole congregation singing the metrical version of the 23rd Psalm and the Abbey choir singing Orlando Gibbons's *Amen*. Its dying notes were picked up by a piper who then played 'The Flo'ers o' the Forest', the traditional Scots lament for Scotland's defeat at Flodden.

Reith would probably have approved of all this, including the *Amen*, and of the blue and white cross of St Andrew, the Saltire, flying from the Abbey tower. He would probably have approved also of his memorial address which was preached not by the Archbishop of Canterbury but by the Moderator of the General Assembly of the Church of Scotland. He compared Reith to David in the Old Testament. He was a man of vision who had never been given a big enough job. He was 'a man who established a kingdom, yet in his heart wanted to build a shrine'. Perhaps the most poignant note in the service came at the beginning when the unaccompanied BBC Chorus sang Purcell's 'Thou knowest Lord, the secrets of our hearts'.

Many of Reith's final obituaries appeared just before or on the day of his memorial service in Westminster Abbey, although the *Financial Times* printed its on the day after his death. Like most obituaries then it was unsigned. It bore the headline 'His ideal for the BBC still untarnished today'. It had little space to qualify this judgement, but it made no effort to simplify it. The obituary was focused almost entirely on his years in the BBC while recognising that he had held many other important offices in his 'long and exceptionally active career', among them Chairman of Imperial Airways. It added that during the war he had held various ministries, including, the barest of statements, Information and Works. No one then or later could learn much from that obituary.

The *Sun*, which published its obituary on the same day, at least gave it a dramatic headline, 'The Tsar who ruled the BBC and clashed with Winston'. Unlike the *Financial Times*, it noted that a lot had changed at Broadcasting House – on the air and off it – 'since the puritanical days of the Reith regime'. The obituary of Reith in *The Times* was the longest, the fullest and, to use Reithian language, the most dignified. One of the shortest, quick to appear, on the same day as *The Times*, was by Peter Black in the *Daily Mail*. It was certainly the least dignified. It was an obituary which annoyed me at the time and still does by its heading, 'The man who WAS Auntie BBC'. I dislike the 'Auntie BBC' designation as much as I dislike the person who designated his first BBC colleagues as uncles in 1922. The practice was followed by Crocombe in the *Radio Times*. Perhaps I shouldn't be so choosy.

In his obituary Peter Black, long-time radio and television critic, who disliked all that Reith represented, fell back on one of the most famous interviews that Reith gave on television – John Freeman's *Face to Face* in 1960. Freeman asked Reith whether, when he ceased to be Director-General, there was anything that he had done while in office that he wished he had not done. After a moment's pause Reith replied 'No'. At the end of this Freeman interview he wrote in his diary that 'the long-dreaded' day had passed off 'entirely well'.

The Times obituary, which covered fully all aspects of Reith's career (including his military service), nevertheless headed it simply 'Creator of British Broadcasting and first BBC Director-General'. 'Reith was destined', wrote its anonymous author, using words Reith would have liked, 'to be a pioneer'. The three ministries he held during the War – Information, Transport, and Works and Buildings, gave him limited scope to do things. Works and Buildings drew him into formulating post-war policies, and it was encouraging that in 1942 all the town and country planning functions of the Ministry of Health were transferred to him. But, and this was the biggest of buts – there were always these – two weeks later Reith ceased to be a minister. Churchill explained curtly, but truly, that he found Reith difficult to work with.

Reith's personal contribution to the war effort now took a new form. He joined the Royal Naval Volunteer Reserve as a lieutenant commander, and in 1942 was promoted to captain. With his love of the Admiralty Churchill would surely have approved of this, but Reith himself saw it as a relegation. In 1946, with the war over and Churchill himself out of office, Reith wrote a remarkable letter to him – how their lives so frequently bounced off each other – complaining that while he held the two ministries that he did under Churchill, the Prime Minister kept himself completely out of touch with him. 'You could have used me in a way and to an extent you never realised.' Attlee, who had been Postmaster-General in Ramsay McDonald's Labour government in 1931, was then Prime Minister, and in 1945 he appointed Reith to an interesting post that was related to Works and Buildings but looked to the future – the chairmanship of the New Towns Committee. Its remit had urgency. It was to lay down principles and formulate procedures. The Committee issued its final report in July 1946, nine months after it had been appointed. Sticking to this renewed preoccupation, early in 1947 Reith became Chairman of the Hemel Hempstead Development Corporation operating within a framework that he himself had devised.

In the same year the BBC launched the Reith Lectures but Reith himself was searching for new and different tasks. In 1950 he became Chairman of the Colonial Development Corporation, a challenging post which he held for nine years and which took him to countries that he had never visited before. Sadly for him it ultimately ended in disillusion. He was told by the Colonial Secretary that he had been in the post long enough and would be replaced.

Throughout the post-war years Reith also held a number of commercial directorates – in the Phoenix Assurance Company, Tube Investments and British Oxygen. I remember vividly his arriving one day by surprise outside my rented Fairholme house in Lewes being driven in a huge British Oxygen car. It was the day of my younger daughter Judith's seventh birthday. Her party was in full swing in the garden, and Reith threw himself into it with abandon, for a time dandling Judith on his knee. It is a memory that she has never forgotten. How different is the way his daughter writes in her account of her life as a child. She described herself in *My Father* as always viewing him from a distance. I did not myself read Marista's book until she gave it to me in 2006.

It is interesting to compare it with a biography of Reith, described as unofficial, by Andrew Boyle *Only the Wind Will Listen: Reith of the BBC*, which I reviewed when it came out in November 1972. It was only the second biography of Reith that had appeared. When Boyle was writing it I tried to give him as much help as Reith had offered me when I was writing *The Birth of Broadcasting*. Boyle was an accomplished biographer, whom I knew well through the BBC, had got to know Reith well, but unfortunately – and foolishly – Reith had given him little help in writing it. In particular, he had given him no access to his diaries.

In my review in the *New Statesman*, which I called 'Without Piety', I recognised that Boyle had been right to focus on Reith's 'theatrical sense'. For all his complex religious stance, grossly over-simplified by Peter Black, but well dealt with by Kenneth Wolfe in his scholarly study, *The Churches and the British Broadcasting Corporation*, no one could have paid less attention than Reith did to the Biblical injunction in Ecclesiastes, 'God is in his heaven and thou upon earth: let thy words be few': *Into the Wind* was a huge, if unselective autobiography. I ended my review of Boyle's biography with what Reith had told me was one of his favourite quotations:

> We must wait till time is exhausted, and we can look back on these scenes of struggle from the realms of security where friendship is everlasting, where the only change is an increase of love and the only rivalry that of benevolence.

Religion in various forms, not only that of the Church of Scotland, had prodded Reith on. Essentially and ultimately, however, it was a source of comfort to him.

One of the most knowledgeable and interesting obituary notices of Reith appeared in *The Listener*, not in 1971 but in 1975 when Charles Stuart's necessarily selective edition of Reith's diaries was published. It was written by Oliver Whitley, who was the son of Reith's most congenial Chairman of the Board of Governors, a former Speaker of the House of Commons, a Nonconformist from Yorkshire, who had been a cotton spinner before going into Liberal politics. When Whitley senior died of cancer after only four years Reith was disconsolate. Flags on all BBC buildings were at half mast and all BBC paper was edged in black for the first time in BBC history.

Oliver, who knew the whole story of Reith from the inside, called him 'a much more extraordinary person than any playwright or novelist would have dared to invent':

> He hated politics but craved for high political office. Irritated about equally by Tories and Socialists he often called himself a Liberal, but he was imperialist, paternalist, authoritarian. Highly critical at times of royalty and the institution of monarchy he constantly aspired to represent it.

This is very well put, but so is a terse entry that Whitley picked up from Reith's diary. 'Extraordinary how completely naturally I slipped into vice-regality'. This was the side of Reith that I liked least. I found the photographs of him as Lord High Commissioner to the Church of Scotland pompous, even offensive. One of the best of them shows John Knox gazing down upon him as he moved into Holyrood. I find offensive too Reith's dismissal, indeed continued relegation into the background, of his wife Muriel, although sadly Knox would have approved of that.

After Reith's death Stuart Hood, whom I had first known when he was head of the BBC's Overseas Service, gave a broadcast in July 1989 on the neglected centenary of Reith's birth that he called 'Yesterday's Man' and which was reprinted in *The Listener*. It was a serious reassessment. 'Great men do not operate in a social vacuum,' he began. 'Reith was a Scot whom a fellow Scot is bound to recognise (with mixed feelings).' He bore the marks of a particular Scottish social formation:

> He sprang from that segment of Scottish society which was dedicated to hard work, to a striving for betterment – a harsh society in which authority, parental or social, enforced respect.

When he founded the BBC 'external circumstances' allowed Reith to achieve the personal objectives which he had formulated as a Scot:

> External Circumstances are very different in the 1980s, but any reassessment of Reith should concentrate on what was positive in his philosophy. Broadcasting is such an immensely important medium that it should not be given over to naked profit-seeking. Access to the broadcasting spectrum carries responsibilities.

I am content to accept this reassessment. It does not date, though we are now living a generation after Hood made it in a very different historical time.

Chapter 5

Abiding Historical Interests

I have never been a strong advocate of studying history in periods, the word usually employed when dividing historical time, although I accept that for undergraduates who are studying history it is helpful, even necessary, to have periods indicated within a history syllabus. They can learn from this what choices are open to them. As a working historian over many years, who fortunately is no longer facing examinations, I prefer to think that the subject of history is best divided up not into dated periods but into continuing strands. These intertwine, and all have loose ends. Some strands attract me more than others and by my own choice – and with no guidance – I seek to stitch or to weave them together.

There are three particular strands which have attracted me since I was a boy at school when almost all my choices were made for me. The first was retailing, the second sport, and the third health. They have attracted me over the years and still do in old age. They are abiding historical interests.

My interest in retailing may well have sprung from my having spent a large part of my boyhood in a family greengrocer's shop connected with my home by a not very wide sloping passage. I knew the word shopping not through going out shopping, which, of course, I did, but by helping to run a shop. I arranged window displays, took customers' orders and put the money they paid me into the till. There were no credit cards, then, although many customers were 'given credit'. Our shop was not on a high street, a now iconic term for local shops struggling to survive in competition with supermarkets. They did not then exist. We had limited competition from shops on the other side of Bradford Road and two far bigger greengrocers' shops 'up town'.

Curiously in my boyhood the main shopping street in Keighley was called not High Street but Low Street. Local topography is always relevant to the organising of retailing. I have vivid memories of Keighley's shops as they were when I was a boy and of the only partially covered market. There my father and other relatives running the business used to buy fruit, vegetables and fish from wholesalers, who bought what they were selling from bigger wholesalers in Bradford and Leeds.

So much has happened to shopkeeping and to shopping since my boyhood, however, that when I now write about retailing I have to discard memory and start with what has been called the biggest change in consumer behaviour since shopkeeping began, the huge increase in online shopping. This can only be described as a retail revolution. Within a quite new context the media have now taken up retailing on an unprecedented scale. Robert Peston has entered the fray.

This is in sharp contrast to the situation even when I started writing *Loose Ends and Extras*. The story of retailing and questions relating to it have been largely left out of history books and, indeed, out of encyclopedias. To dig deeper you have to turn to the biographies of 'great retailers'. And these were few. Thomas Lipton and Gordon Selfridge were picked out largely for what they did outside their shops rather than for what they accomplished in them. One exception to the rule was Alison Adburgham's *Shops and Shopping* (1964). As a fashion journalist she followed her own way into retailing history. Her book covered the long period from 1800 to the beginning of the Great War in 1914.

Nevertheless, Alison had two things in common with me. Having written for *Punch* in 1961, she published *The Punch History of Manners and Modes*, which was a very different and less serious book than *Cap and Bell*, which my wife and I co-edited in 1973. My connection with *Punch* is that I knew Bill Davies, the editor, who had a flat in Brighton. The second thing Alison and I had in common was that we both wrote for the *Manchester Guardian*, then edited by A. P. Wadsworth. I knew him well, and he invited me to write articles and reviews for him. We shared an interest in nineteenth-century history and whenever I was in Manchester I used to be invited into his office, never to discuss the day's news but always nineteenth-century history. He told his secretary not to disturb us until he told her.

Alison was more bold than me. Not knowing Wadsworth, she approached him by post, suggesting that she should write a fortnightly column on fashion for the *Manchester Guardian*. He took up the idea willingly, although he was personally uninterested in fashion and preferred writing on Sunday schools to writing on what Victorians called 'milliners' shops'. Alison was pleased that in consequence photographs were not mentioned at all when they met. All the three books on retailing which I have subsequently written have depended on them.

The first of them was *Friends of the People*, a centenary history of the business established by David Lewis, an enterprising and colourful Jewish shopkeeper who leased his first shop in Ranelagh Street, Liverpool in 1856. He had arrived in Liverpool, hoping to make a fortune, in 1839. His first shop was a modest one, but between 1856 and his death in 1885 he leased more shops around his – in face of unpleasant competition – and added new departments to his own store. He was not following any strategic plan but only one criterion: 'Will it pay?' Lewis also acquired a second store in Liverpool to which he gave the Parisian name Bon Marché 'after the convenient and large Paris shop whose only drawback was that it was always full!' Down to the outbreak of the Great War, that is almost thirty years after Lewis's death, Bon Marché delivery vans in Liverpool were painted in the same striped colours as those of the Bon Marché in Paris.

As a businessman David believed in bulk purchase and high turnover. Everything would be sold at the smallest profit. But he widened the range of goods that he was selling. Thus, in 1874 the local press noted that women's and girls' shoes were selling in large quantities. Five years later Lewis added tobacco, cigars and pipes for men.

Advertising was crucial to his success. In 1893 a local Liverpool paper claimed that the city had 'never seen an advertiser who even approached Mr. Lewis in novel devices and judiciously large expenditure'. Among his advertisements I particularly liked one for football. 'Everything for the game', not just 'football outfits'. The second of my abiding historical interests covered in this chapter is the history of sport, itself a more complex subject than the history of retailing.

Lewis had a strong sense of history also, and he put this to good use in 1880 when he reissued *Gorer's Liverpool Directory* of 1790 which depicted on its covers an illustration of his Ranelagh Street shop. On a different plane, from December 1882 onwards he published a series of *Penny Readings* consisting of *Selections from the Best Poets, Prose Writers and Best Speakers, together with Miscellaneous and Original Literary Compositions*. The first two issues contained a compact account of his own life.

Thereafter his *Penny Readings* spoke for themselves, drawing out two good Victorian morals. First, no word would appear in them that would 'serve as an apology for vice' and 'bring a blush to the cheek of a modest woman'. Second, each copy of the *Readings* made the claim that it 'was a lesson in THRIFT: it costs only a penny'. In current perspectives thrift has nothing to do with consumerism. Lewis had no use for *isms*. By the time that he produced his *Penny Readings* he was a sick man living not in Liverpool but in Southport, where he died in his home in 1885 at the age of sixty-two.

On his death he was succeeded by a nephew, Louis Cohen, who had become his partner in 1871. He had not bequeathed the business to Louis who had to acquire it from his own accumulated funds. Prudent and secretive, Louis's personal qualities were quite different from David's. Nevertheless, he was responsible for arranging what was possibly the biggest of Lewis's advertising exploits. While David was dying Louis chartered the most famous of all steamships, Brunel's *Great Eastern*, which had been put up for auction, and converted it after a perilous journey from Milford Haven to Liverpool into a large floating advertisement. It incorporated a shooting gallery, toffee stalls, an American bar and a photographic studio. On its starboard side it announced that 'Lewis's Ranelagh Street, Liverpool, Manchester and Birmingham' – the last two of them new Lewis's stores – 'are THE FRIENDS OF THE PEOPLE'.

Most important in the history of Lewis's, Cohen had a remarkably strong family sense, and Cohens – there were many of them – ran the business and continued to run it after it became a public company in 1904, Lewis Ltd. In January the *Drapery Times*, without once mentioning Lewis's advertising, observed that,

> the constant growth of this store from small beginnings to its present magnitude represents the triumph of a fair and honest business policy which has won the public confidence and appreciation among countless thousands of well informed and intelligent shoppers in the Liverpool and North Wales district.

My book, *Friends of the People*, the title of which I derived from the advertisement, ended with the year 1954. I completed it in 1955, and it was published in 1956. Between these two dates I had got married, and Susan and I had moved from Oxford to Leeds. There in Leeds was an imposing new Lewis's store designed by a Leeds architect who had visited the United States looking at department stores there before he completed his design. He visited shopping malls and early supermarkets. There was nothing particularly Leodensian in his Leeds store which was located not in a mall but on a broad new road, the Headrow.

This stretched westward from Leeds's great Victorian town hall, opened in 1858, about which I was to write much, drawing on precious, hitherto-unused local sources. These were of a range and depth missing in the largely war-destroyed Lewis's archives. The town hall, paid for from local rates, was opened by Queen Victoria accompanied by the Prince Consort. They arrived by train and were met by an impressive welcoming party which included Earl Fitzwilliam and the Bishop of Ripon. They were driven then by carriage to Woodsley House, the home of the Mayor, Peter Fairbairn, a self-made man. Flags and banners were everywhere and medals were struck in great numbers. Tickets for the town hall were in great demand. The Chief Constable of Leeds had an augmented police force under his command, and the military was present in strength. The Queen and Prince Consort watched a huge Sunday School demonstration presented by (very precisely) 32,110 children. After the royal party reached the town hall a magnificent organ pealed out the National Anthem, and when that had been sung the Bishop of Ripon said prayers and the Hallelujah Chorus was sung.

Music was an integral part of the festivities; a musical festival was to follow the opening and Mendelssohn's *Elijah* was sung by a great choir. After I left Leeds I was to associate it more with music than with shops. In 1963 Fanny Waterman co-founded with Marion Lascelles, as she then was, the Leeds International Pianoforte Competition. It thrives.

When I lived in Leeds I used to go past Lewis's Headrow store by tram every weekday on the way to and from home to the University, where I was the only historian to be in any way interested in retail history. I travelled not along the Headrow but up and down the much older Leeds street, Briggate, passing on the way the great Victorian Grand Theatre, opened in 1879. Just to the west of Briggate was Leeds's magnificent Victorian covered market which we took all visitors to see and where we used to shop more often than we did in Lewis's.

I love great Victorian covered markets, which stimulate my imagination, not least when they are in great foreign cities. That in Bombay, which I enjoyed going around stall by stall with an Indian friend, I once had the special privilege of gazing down upon from above. I was taken there by the market manager – he had a grand title which I have forgotten – who appreciated my desire to get to know everything I could about the building in his charge. It was an experience which I shall never forget.

I have written and broadcast often not only about the great covered markets that I love, but about street markets. I always used to enjoy walking through them. I recall – and these are only examples –

London's Brick Lane, the innumerable street markets in Paris, and the market in Accra, Ghana, where famous marketwomen delight in giving you all the news of the city as well as all the gossip. When we moved back from Sussex to Oxford in 1976 I came to appreciate Oxford's small covered market in the heart of the city. I knew it, too, stall by stall, and the particular stalls where I could buy fruit, vegetables, fish and fowls, cheeses and everything else that I wanted.

Returning as I must to Lewis's, the first non-Cohen to join the management of the company, F. J. Marquis, had entered the business in 1920, two years before Louis Cohen's death, and he was immediately placed on the board of the company along with four Cohens. By 1939 he was Chairman and Managing Director and, raised to the peerage as Lord Woolton, he was to be Churchill's Minister of Food until 1943. I got to know Woolton quite well and greatly to respect him. Of humble birth, he was a boy at Manchester Grammar School and a student at Manchester University. His first job was Senior Mathematics Master at Burnley Grammar School.

I saw most of Woolton after the Second World War when, without abandoning politics, he returned to retailing at Lewis's. He became Chairman and Joint Managing Director of the company in 1950. In the following landmark year a huge step which can be described as 'historic' was taken when Lewis Ltd moved from the provinces where it had originated and blossomed, and acquired Selfridges in London. This had been founded by Gordon Selfridge, as much of a showman as David Lewis had been. The subject of a current television series, he had to leave his Oxford Street store in 1941 because his funds had run out. They had often threatened to do that. Marquis had once told him years before then that Lewis's would one day take over his store, but that he was prepared to wait.

I knew that before Selfridge arrived in London he had worked in Marshall Field's great pioneering store in Chicago. An American friend of mine, Ronald Tree, belonged to the founding family and made a fortune out of the business. I often stayed with him and his wife Marietta in his beautiful Palladian-style house in Barbados, the Caribbean Island to which he retired and to the welfare of which he was to contribute much. He is a link figure in *Loose Ends and Extras*, for he had placed his authentically old English house, Ditchley Park, at the disposal of Winston Churchill during the Second World War. It was a perfect retreat for the Prime Minister and much secret business was transacted there.

My third book on retailing, a centennial history of Marks and Spencer, as famous as Selfridges but with no American element in its history, was written at the invitation of my friend Marcus Sieff, later Lord Sieff. Since it was to be read only by men and women working for M&S, it was never reviewed. There was only one history of M&S that had been reviewed, that written by Goronwy Rees, *St. Michael: A History of Marks and Spencer*, published in 1969. Its content attracted less attention than the controversial character of its author. I liked his book and the name that he gave to it, *St. Michael*. This was M&S's brand name and the name of the house journal, *St. Michael's News*, which I used as a valuable source for my own book. Only now as I write this chapter have I noted that all my books on retailing have been centennial histories.

The founder of M&S's business was Michael Marks, born in Slonim in the Russian Polish province of Grodno in 1859. His mother died in giving him birth. He came to England as a refugee from one of the many Tsarist pogroms – in Russian *pogrom* means destruction – and started life in this country as an itinerant peddler in the north-east of Yorkshire or in adjacent Durham. We do not know the exact place or the exact time when he began to sell his goods on a trestle table in an open market in Leeds. The first authenticated date in his English life was that of his marriage in 1886 to Hannah Cohen, then twenty-one years old. The name Cohen, the family name of David Lewis's successors, is a Jewish name with priestly/kingly origins. In his marriage licence Michael is described as a 'licensed hawker'.

The first Marks child died in infancy. Their second, Simon, was to become chairman of the M&S company, founded in 1903, and was to remain chairman for nearly fifty years. The first Michael had died in 1907. In 1894 he had acquired a permanent stall in the great covered market in Leeds, which was opened in 1857, and in that year he took on as a partner a man whom he knew to be a first-class bookkeeper, Tom Spencer, born in Skipton, Yorkshire, in 1851, the year of the Great Exhibition in the Crystal Palace. Skipton, further up the Aire Valley, was Keighley's neighbouring town. My mother who was a Spencer before she married my father and long survived him, used to claim that Tom was a distant relative.

Marks and Spencer created one of the most famous business partnerships in history, rivalling in fame that between Matthew Boulton and James Watt in eighteenth-century Birmingham. M&S, however, was a quite differently based partnership. It stood out because it was a partnership between a Jew and a Gentile. It lasted until Spencer died in 1905. Two years earlier M&S had become a limited liability company with shareholders. It had gone far since the day when Michael placed a notice on his goods on display in Leeds market 'Don't ask the price. It's a penny'.

Michael also opened penny stalls in Wakefield and Castleford. His first business slogan had worked, and he decided to move his head-quarters and his home across the Pennines to Manchester, spending three years in Wigan on the way. His Manchester penny bazaar was far more imposing than his home. The slogan 'Don't Ask the Price. It's a penny' was printed in scarlet across the front with the words 'Admission Free' added. It was the prototype for a widely dispersed group of M&S penny bazaars. In 1897 a separate warehouse was acquired near Strangeways Prison and in 1901 a new warehouse built to the partners' design.

When I wrote my centennial history I had as little documentary evidence to work on as when I was writing *Friends of the People*, and I was excited to find two small penny notebooks that had survived, one labelled 'Mr. Marks', the other 'Mr. Spencer', which set out the details of the trading fortunes of the two partners from 1894 to January 1898. In three years their initial capital of £759 15 shillings and 11 pence (how precise!) had increased to £5,000 net. Two years later M&S was running penny bazaars in twenty-three towns and branch establishments in eleven other places, including Bath, Birmingham, Wolverhampton, Middlesbrough and Hartlepool. The last of these was the place where Michael had probably landed on his arrival from Russia as a refugee. In 1897 he was naturalised as a British subject. A landmark date in company history was 1904 when M&S acquired premises in Leeds in the recently opened Cross Arcade, not far from its later store.

In 1909, the year that Selfridge opened his store in Oxford Street, London, Leeds' *Shoppers' Guide* stated proudly – and correctly – that 'no city in England can boast a more wonderful transformation than that witnessed in Leeds during the last two or three decades. The centre of Leeds has been practically recarved and polished.' M&S then had no fewer than seven London stores, although none of them were in central London.

I ended my centennial history perhaps surprisingly with a chapter on philosophy, which was preceded by chapters on folklore and performance. Leaving symbolism, a tricky subject, on one side, I noted how Marcus Sieff, the friend who had commissioned me to write the book, liked to insist on the important role of the practical philosophy that had not only laid the foundations of the family business but had made it grow. It had been formulated by Simon Marks and Israel Sieff, who first met in Manchester in 1901, and it rested on six principles. I am always drawn to the number six, two times three. It reminds me of the Six Points propounded by the Chartists in the 1830s and 1840s. It was also the number of the Hut where I worked in Bletchley Park.

The first M&S principle was to offer customers under the brand name St Michael a selective range of products and prices. The second was to encourage suppliers to use the most modern and efficient techniques of production provided by the latest discoveries in science and technology. The third was to enforce with the cooperation of these suppliers the highest standards of quality control, and the fourth was to plan the expansion of the stores for the better display of a widening range of goods 'for the convenience of our customers'. The fifth was to simplify operating procedures so that the business was carried on in an efficient manner, and the sixth was to foster good human relations between customers, suppliers and staff.

While the distinctive identity of each M&S store depended on its location, the managers of all M&S stores were expected to embrace and adhere to a common M&S philosophy. Like Simon Marks and Israel Sieff, who had been exact contemporaries at Manchester Grammar School, with each in later life marrying the other's sister, M&S staff at all levels, not just managers, often had a strong family sense which they proudly proclaimed. Thus, at the Winchester branch, Frank Bailey, a warehouseman, described how deeply involved his family was in the local business. His married sister was the staff manageress, another sister was an invoice clerk, and a third sister was a junior window dresser. At a bus stop on their way to the store neighbours would call out 'There goes the M&S platoon.'

I have a taste for such significant detail when I write history, and I like to write what Edward Thompson taught me to call history from below. It was I who discovered from the surviving M&S archives that the Baileys constituted one-seventh of the total M&S work force in Winchester. I also believe, however, as I am not sure that Edward did, that a historian should never ignore history from above. I was fascinated to learn that when the manager of the Hull/Bridlington M&S store retired in 1982 Lord Sieff telephoned him to wish him well on his retirement.

Two Lord Sieffs, Marcus and Israel – Simon Marks had been the first M&S peer – chose in their maiden speeches in the Lords to talk about human relations, the last of the Six Principles enunciated by Simon and Israel. They insisted on using this term, never speaking inside or outside the Lords of industrial relations as most political leaders did and do and as professors of industrial relations, of whom I have known many, always do. Yet their language could seem a touch complacent. None of the Sieffs dwell too long on the fact that when *St. Michael's News* advertised that M&S policy was to sell goods made in Britain and that 96 per cent of their goods on sale were so made, a necessary corollary was that they enjoyed what economists call monopsonistic power over their suppliers. Marcus encouraged me, nevertheless, to travel to the factories of their suppliers, to examine their modes of production and to meet and talk to their operatives. One of them was in Keighley.

I did not know that in 1975 M&S would open a great store in Paris where it would not have been politic to make too much of the slogan that M&S sold goods made in Britain. In 1968, when Paris was torn apart by troubles, *les événements*, M&S had acquired a very English coat of arms. A lion represented England and an owl wisdom. Together they supported a symbol of the Archangel Michael. A pair of golden scales portrayed justice and fair trading. White roses represented Yorkshire where Michael Marks had set up his stall on a trestle table. A ladder of the type figuring in Jacob's dream was a sign of Michael's aspiration and will to prosper. A horn of plenty represented plenitude of goods (not all of them British). Beneath the crest was the motto 'Strive, probe, apply', a threesome I have seen nowhere else.

When Marcus Sieff had joined the M&S board in 1954 his first task had been to take charge of the food department which under his direction increased its share of total M&S sales from 14 per cent in 1956 to over 25 per cent in 1963. This strengthening of the share was perhaps Marcus's chief legacy to the business. With food can go wine, although M&S did not sell it until 1973 and then only with an initial range of five wines and four sherries. In 1986, when I began to write my centennial history, the range of wines had risen to 51, and sales of wines had risen from £0.1 million to £35 million. Wine or perhaps grapes might have been shown somewhere on any new M&S coat of arms.

I was particularly interested in this impressive rise in the sales of wine for in 1985 I had brought out my second book on retailing, *Wine for Sale: Victoria Wine and the Liquor Trade*, which like *Friends of the People* was published by Batsford. It had a good story to tell. It proceeded from the bold initiative of Eric Colwell, whom I had got to know well when I chaired one of several Node courses where promising young businessmen and young civil servants met in parallel groups to discuss problems that were of mutual interest. After dinner far older businessmen addressed them. Marcus Sieff was one of them. The story of Victoria Wine is a good story. Walter Winch Hughes had started his Victoria Wine business in Mark Lane in the City of London in 1865, and by the time he died in 1886, shortly after my centennial history of M&S began, there were no fewer than ninety-eight shops in what had become the first of Britain's wine shop chains. Their locations stretched from Bristol to Norwich and from Birmingham to Brighton, and many of their local stores were photographed. The photographs were a part of my evidence. Some stores were destroyed during the Second World War.

The story of what happened to Victoria Wine in the century after 1886 enthralled me as it did the best-selling writer on wine, Hugh Johnson, whose *Pocket Wine Book* was first published in 1977. Auberon Waugh, a *bon viveur* whom I knew and liked, described my *Wine for Sale* as 'simply indispensable for all wine drinkers, however grand or however poor'. In 1984 he had observed that the production of books about wine had now outstripped the growth in wine consumption. As women were buying increasing numbers of cookery books men were finding that laying down a wine library could be almost as interesting as laying down a cellar.

I was fortunate in persuading John Arlott, 'man of Hampshire', perhaps the greatest cricket commentator of all time, to write a foreword to my *Wine for Sale*. He collected books as well as wines and at his Hampshire house had a specialised collection of topographical books that he bought cheaply in London street markets. I enjoyed talking to him about them almost as much as I enjoyed drinking his superb wines. I was sad when he moved from Hampshire to Alderney in the Channel Islands, an island with a far longer history than Victoria Wine and even than Hampshire Cricket Club.

It was not easy in that small island to distinguish between Roman and Nazi fortifications. I had other reasons for going to Alderney, for I was invited to write a history of the German occupation of the islands for the jubilee of their liberation in 1945. It was an absorbing commission to undertake with many echoes and many ramifications. Exeter College, Oxford, again came into my big picture. As a boy of sixteen Peter Crill, later Sir Peter Crill, Bailiff of Guernsey, escaped from the island by boat in November 1944 and landed on the Normandy coast at the start of a journey to Oxford, bicycling all the way from Weymouth. He wanted to get an undergraduate place. They first said there was no place. In Exeter College, however, the Rector, crossing the quad and noticing his bicycle clips, asked him how far he had travelled. Greatly impressed by Peter's energy and ambition he offered him a place at once.

In pursuing my abiding interest in retailing, not only in Lewis's, M&S and Victoria Wine, I was fortunate in knowing, sometimes very well, people who kept me continually involved with it. My friend and pupil at Worcester, John Sainsbury, was the most important of them, and he and his brother Tim, who was MP for Hove from 1973, when I was still Vice-Chancellor of Sussex, to 1997, were the biggest benefactors Worcester College has ever had. As an undergraduate in Cambridge at Sidney Sussex College I had been a good customer of the wonderful Sainsbury retail store, conveniently near to the College, and I felt that it was the best retail shop I had ever seen.

John was a super-retailer in an age of supermarkets, and I recall with pleasure trips across the Channel with him and his wife, the former ballet dancer Anya Lindon, and my wife Susan visiting places in France which we particularly wanted to see and vineyards where the Sainsburys bought and kept their wines. John was as much of a *bon viveur* as Ned Sherrin, a special tribute to them both. I owe a very special debt indeed to John also. Since I wrote the second volume of this trilogy, *Special Relationships*, he has endowed a Fellowship in perpetuity in my name at Worcester College. There is no honour that I have been paid that I appreciate as much. John and I had a very special relationship with the architect Richard McCormack who designed wonderful new buildings for the College, overlooking the lake in the grounds.

One of John Sainsbury's great admirers was my neighbour in Tyninghame House, Alistair Grant. We acquired a share in Tyninghame after I retired from the Provostship of Worcester. He and Judy were the first pair to move in there after the house had been converted. In 1986 Alistair had become Chief Executive of Safeway and in 1993 its Chairman. Safeway stores were diverse in scale, range of customers and profitability, and Alistair learned much about them by 'dropping into' a store as Marcus Sieff did. It was not Marcus, however, who was his hero, but John Sainsbury. I dropped into the Safeway store in Orkney with Alistair when he and Judy visited Orkney with Susan and me. I confess that I remember that store less well than meeting in an Orkney pub, not for the first time, Seamus Heaney, a poet I admire immensely. I had been one of his sponsors when he was elected Professor of Poetry in Oxford.

Tragically Alistair died in his prime in 2001, just as he was about to become Governor of the Bank of Scotland. It was the same year when, in Portugal, I was stricken with deep-vein thrombosis. Judy provided a car to take me to Edinburgh to speak at his memorial service in St Giles. I had to be assisted to climb the stairs up to the pulpit. I never thought that I could do so, as I wrote in the second volume of this trilogy, which I could never have written and published without Judy's generous support. As I looked down from the pulpit across the crowded pews I meditated on why I was alive and a dear friend far younger than me was dead.

My interest in retailing remains as strong in 2014 as it ever was. I have a large collection of press cuttings which keep me up to date. In particular, I watch the changing fortunes of M&S almost as meticulously as I did when Marcus Sieff was alive. I note with interest that Sir David Sieff, the last member of the founding family to sit as an executive director of the M&S board from 1972 to 1997 and as a non-executive director for four years after that, retiring in 2001, is returning home as director of the M&S archive and museum. These are located in the Parkinson Building on the University of Leeds campus. The present Chief Executive of M&S is a Dutchman, appointed in May 2010, and its Chairman since December 2010 has been Robert Swannell, an investment banker. Food is still its business staple. The company sold more mince pies at Christmas 2013 than any other retailer.

M&S is not one of the 'big four' supermarkets, Tesco, Asda, Sainsbury's and Morrisons, all of whom have had their recent ups and downs. Tesco's market share remains the greatest, and Sainsbury's has risen to second place under an outstanding chief executive, Justin

King, appointed in 2003. While I was in the last stages of writing *Loose Ends and Extras* he handed in his resignation. This surprised the media. Meanwhile the big four face competition from up-market Waitrose, owned by the John Lewis Partnership, which is opening a small showplace shop at Heathrow when the Queen's Terminal opens in the summer of 2014. The Partnership played a part in Bletchley Park, which I explain in the first volume of this trilogy, *Secret Days*. The big four face competition also from two German supermarkets, Aldi and Lidl. Aldi, which arrived in Britain in the 1990s, opened its 500th store in Bury St Edmunds, which figures in a quite different context in the last chapter of *Loose Ends*. In its own context it has made its founder, Karl Albrecht, aged ninety, the richest man in Germany. Retailing never stands still even in Lewes. A Safeway store was turned into a Waitrose, and Tesco, once dominant, faces a challenge from Aldi.

Loyalty cards were said to be the secret of Tesco's supremacy in the 1990s. Loyalties can be fickle in retailing. In sport, the second strand in my historical interests, they are as abiding as my historical interests are. Manchester United under Sir Alex Ferguson won loyal supporters in all parts of the world, including Iran, where an unauthorised edition of *Alex Ferguson: My Autobiography*, launched in October 2013, became one of the best- and fastest-selling books of the year. On the BBC *Today* programme Nick Robinson, the BBC's Political Editor, called Ferguson 'one of the greatest living Britons' and it was widely asked by journalists whether his insights would help in the business world. I have never been a supporter of Manchester United, but I see the relevance of the question. Since I lived in Leeds in the golden age of Don Revie I have been loyal to Leeds United, then a great team but now exactly half-way up the Championship league table. With these big gates, and their loyal supporters, they have never provided a business model.

The leading soccer star early in Revie's time was John Charles, a great centre-forward. I remember a strange day when the Duke of Edinburgh came to open a new university building and I had to be present. I could not get to the hospital in Bramley where my wife was about to have a baby. I rushed there by taxi to find out if the baby had arrived and found that the nurses were talking only of the arrival of John Charles's son. He was the heaviest baby that they had ever seen. Only then did I see my own first child, who was of normal weight. She was a girl and Susan and I had chosen the name Katharine for her. Susan had had difficulties at her own christening. Her mother wanted to call her Judith, but the vicar told her that he would not allow her to call her baby that. What would she call her? In confusion her mother gabbled out 'Susan'. There were no difficulties, of course, with Katharine. I believed that her name should be spelled with a capital K and an 'a' in the middle, not an 'e'. We called our next daughter Judith.

My interest in sport, like my interest in retailing, leads me back to my childhood. I used to play rugby union at school but watch rugby league at Lawkholme Lane, where I also watched Bradford League cricket. It was also the place where my school had its annual sports day and from which we started our long-distance runs across the moors. Lawkholme Lane had become the home of the cricket and football clubs in 1883 and the rugby club started to play there in 1885. The cricket club did not join the Bradford League until 1916. Neither of the Keighley clubs was particularly successful.

I have a souvenir programme of a bazaar organised by the two clubs in 1933 in which it is stated clearly that honours in rugby league have 'thus far avoided Keighley'. In 1937, however, for the only time in its history, Keighley Rugby League Club won a place in the cup final at Wembley. I went with them, one of thousands of supporters, to watch them play against Widnes. They lost. That was the only time before the Second World War that I went to what I must now call Old Wembley. It was an event I can never forget.

I have subsequently read a lot about rugby league history, and the changing relationship between thirteen-man rugby league and fifteen-man rugby union. It is interesting that the Keighley club had started by playing rugby union, its first match being against Crosshill, then a small village between Keighley and Skipton, in 1876. The Rugby Union had been brought into existence five years before. The Football Association concerned with what is now universally known as soccer, was formed in 1863, and it is interesting that the Rugby Union was established in the same year as the inaugural FA Challenge Cup Final.

The game as played at Rugby School supposedly began when William Webb Ellis 'first took the ball in his arms and ran with it, thus originating the distinctive feature of the rugby game'. There is a memorial tablet to him at Rugby School, erected in February 1900. Northern rugby became a mass spectator sport, a future which could never have been foreseen in Rugby School, with the Yorkshire Cup final after 1893 attracting average audience of over 15,000. In the south of England, however, Rugby Union still looked back to the game as it was played at Rugby School. There was a distrust of big crowds, especially working-class crowds at a time of growing industrial unrest. Cup competitiveness had little appeal in the south. At the Rugby Union's annual meeting in September 1893 a Yorkshire proposal that players 'be allowed compensation for bona fide loss of time' was defeated. As a result, in August 1895, twenty-two clubs seceded from the Rugby Union to form the Northern Rugby Union. By 1898 they numbered ninety-eight. This break has come to be called 'the Great Schism'.

One of the most interesting features of sport, always used in the singular in Britain, whereas the Americans always refer to sports, is the appeal to history. In *The Victorians and Sport* (2004) Mike Huggins drew on a mass of Victorian monographs and articles. In his preface he begins with sport at the beginning of Queen Victoria's reign when it was closely identified with field sports, especially hunting, fowling and fishing. By the end of the reign there had been something like a revolution in the scale and nature of sport. Other sports, apart from soccer and rugby which I have already mentioned, such as golf and tennis, became popular. Sport could cause divisions for different social groups who approached their sports in very different ways. Some involved women. Some had stars such as the jockey Fred Archer and the cricketer W. G. Grace. Gambling had been an accompaniment of sport, particularly horse racing and prize fighting, before Queen Victoria came to the throne. There was no sense then, however, of a national sporting calendar. There were big events like Derby Day and there were religious, seasonal and regional calendars covering local events.

By the beginning of the twentieth century there was a national sporting calendar and the media paid increasing attention to it. There was now an emphasis on leisure as well as recreation. Nevertheless there was still a regular appeal to history: the remembrance of old games and old sporting heroes. The word 'historic' is used more in sport than it is in almost any other context. The context of sport, however, is always changing and consequently, in studying its history, we confront the basic historical problem of the relationship between continuity and change. While I am writing this chapter tributes have been paid to one famous soccer player, Sir Tom Finney, who played for Preston North End. There is a statue to him at Deepdale, the Preston North End ground. In 2000 Finney went with a hundred thousand others to Stoke for the funeral of his great friend and contemporary Sir Stanley Matthews.

Like Matthews, Finney was a man of grace, dignity and unyielding integrity. He was offered huge riches to join Italian club Palermo but stayed in Preston where he earned £12 a week. He was never once booked in his career or sent off. Jimmy Greaves, the former Chelsea, Tottenham Hotspur and England forward, said of him:

> When I was a boy, Tom Finney was a hero of mine. All these years on nothing has changed. He was not only a maker, but a taker of goals. Above all he was a gentleman player who never retaliated, irrespective of how shabby the treatment meted out to him. And, believe me, back in those days it was a very combative and physical game compared to today.

For one season-ticket holder at Deepdale, he was the player who made Preston 'proud'. Finney never won an FA Cup final medal: the closest he came to winning one of football's major prizes was in the 1954 Cup Final which Preston lost to West Bromwich Albion. Finney retired in 1960, having played 433 League games.

The name lawn tennis was coined by Major Wingfield, late 1st Dragoon Guards. It was first played in the 1870s. With the codification of the rules, the inauguration and development in 1877 of the Wimbledon Championships was an impetus to the game. The United States Lawn Tennis Association was set up in 1881, but it was not until 1888 that the Lawn Tennis Association was set up in England. It was a sport in which from the start women played as active a part as men. Through the last two decades of the nineteenth century *The Field* published an annual lawn tennis calendar, a fascinating conjunction of two very different sports. Lawn tennis has produced a contemporary British Wimbledon champion, Andy Murray, the first to win since Fred Perry before the war. Lawn tennis was soon very much an international sport. In 1900 the International Lawn Tennis Championship, now known as the Davis Cup, was inaugurated.

As in the case of most sports, broadcasting, first radio and then television, has had an enormous influence on the way games are played and reported. Radio broadcasting of Wimbledon began as early as 1937. There is a close connection between money supplied through the media and the rules of sport. The decision makers in sport have found it easier to change the rules of their sports to appeal to the demands of television rather than those of live spectators. Some sports also changed the timing of their games as a result of television.

The economics of sport are as intricate as the publicity given to it through the media. Transfer deals, now international, are a feature of soccer. There is a so-called transfer window in January. The total amount of money spent by English Premier League clubs in 2014 has been £129.6 million. In 2013 it was £123 million, in 2012 £65 million, and in 2010 £30 million. Players are loaned as well as bought and sold. There has been public interest in, and public opposition to, the enormous transfer fees of players and the sums they earn in wages and through their business activities outside sport altogether. David Beckham, a player of talent, stands out as a highly successful businessman.

Former Archbishop Carey confessed recently that he was a loyal Arsenal supporter. and in an interview pointed out that many of the first soccer teams were founded by Sunday schools and other religious organisations. Everton was one such club. Others were Manchester City, Aston Villa, Bolton Wanderers and Tottenham Hotspur. Carey ended by saying that the great danger of contemporary soccer was greed. The *Guardian/Observer* had listed this first in a series of seven deadly sins of football. The third was wrath.

The involvement of all media, new and old, in sport was as significant as religion in sporting history, but then for many observers the media itself had become a religion, as indeed sport had become.

My own interest in sport and its history was as well known in Australia and the United States as it was in Britain. At the time of the Sydney Olympics of 2000 I was invited to give Flack Lectures on the history of sport by the runner Herb Elliot. The brochure advertising my lecture, 'Sport and the Historian', noted that sport's appeal is often compared with that of religion but 'winning and losing is more immediate'. So are statistics.

It is interesting that there are as many links between statistics and sport as there are between religion and sport. Cricket in particular makes the very most of historical statistics and *Wisden Cricketers' Almanac*, which sticks to unadorned facts, provides statistics which are picked up by commentators in all the media.

Retailing, religion and statistics provide links with the third of my abiding interests, health. A former M&S boss, Sir Stuart Rose, took on the challenge of 'turning around' the NHS, which figured as much in the daily newspapers, radio and television as sport. I have described in this chapter how the first two of my three abiding interests take me back into my boyhood. Of my third abiding interest I cannot quite say the same. As a boy I had every conceivable illness before the age of ten, including a spell with diphtheria in a scarlet fever hospital. I also knew friends of mine who lived in the same street who suffered terribly from the serious side-effects of familiar illnesses. One girl I knew became blind as a by-product of measles. I started wearing glasses at the age of ten and the fact that I wore them stopped me from getting into the Navy when war broke out, which would have been my preference. As it was, I went into the Army graded A1. I had got rid of my illnesses for much of the rest of my life.

It was after the Second World War that I really began to be interested in health. By now a professional historian, I wrote my first two articles in *The Times* on the centenary of the passing of the Public Health Act of 1848. I gave my first post-war lecture in Leicester to the Chadwick Trust on 'Public Opinion and Public Health in the Age of Chadwick'. My growing interest in public health owed much to Sammy Finer, one of my colleagues at the Formation College near Bedford to which I moved after leaving Bletchley Park. We used to talk about public health together, and he himself wrote a most interesting book on Chadwick. My lectures on William Beveridge and full employment after the war were a topical complement, given Beveridge's own interests, rather than a diversion.

The most important contribution I made to health studies after the end of the war was writing the fourth volume in a history of the Royal College of Physicians of London. The first three volumes had been published in 1964, 1966 and 1972 respectively and covered the history of the College from its foundation in 1518 to 1947 where I took up the story. It made it a very different volume from the other three. I devoted far more space in it to a biographical study of Fellows of the College based on a series of obituaries published by the College under the title *Munk's Roll*. These volumes were named after Dr William Munk, Harveian Librarian for forty years, from 1857 until 1898.

In the background of my own fourth volume was of course the formation of the National Health Service and through following the subsequent history of the NHS I have kept myself fully up to date with what is going on, achievements and problems. The Second World War had quickened the demand for a comprehensive National Health Service and I had its origins in mind when I wrote my articles in *The Times* on the centenary of the Public Health Act of 1848. It was interesting for me to examine the whole changing relationship between private health and public health and I have supervised graduate students writing theses on aspects of this, one of them dealing not with the United Kingdom but with Sweden.

I have had one other interesting post-war commitment involving the history of health, when I was asked to write a history of the Bethlem asylum and worked on it in the Royal Maudsley Hospital. I found this a formidable assignment, and while I did not produce a published volume I do not regret the amount of time I spent carrying out that primary research. It was not until 1997 that the *History of Bethlem* appeared in the heaviest book (literally) which I have ever been involved with, co-edited with Jonathan Andrews, Roy Porter, who became a great friend, Penny Tucker and Keir Waddington, who did more than any of the rest of us to see the book through the press.

Bethlem had moved in 1783 to a handsome new building which is now the Imperial War Museum, where I have spent much of my time working on matters totally unrelated to health. In our composite volume I was mainly concerned with the very last part of the *History of Bethlem*. At the end of the volume I asked,

> What is it that makes institutions perpetuate themselves, assume a life of their own? And how does that affect those associated with them in the shorter term? An institution like Bethlem has gone through phases of inertia and momentum and those connected with it outside have largely effected the direction it took in each phase.

Since our volume appeared, as in the case of retailing and sport, I keep myself up to date by reading the press regularly and by collecting press cuttings.

Every day there are letters to the press dealing with NHS management. One in the *Daily Telegraph* followed a letter from David Nunn asserting that the NHS needed to be run by those who understand healthcare, not shopping. In reply Mike Perridge from Lincoln, wrote,

> The NHS needs to be run by those who know how to manage, a quality Sir Stuart Rose has clearly demonstrated. Too often it is assumed that a good practitioner will make a good manager without any further training. One would never allow an outstanding hospital manager to practice medicine, so why look only to medical practitioners to manage the NHS?

There is far more interest in matters such as dementia, 'the biggest health issue we face', and in cancer than I ever would have anticipated when the NHS was founded. Smoking was once one of these. They figure in headlines as do organisational questions such as the role of Accident and Emergency Departments in hospitals, the number of beds in the wards and scandals in the provision of health care. The culture of health care, a term used increasingly, was often described as 'chilling'. The Health Minister, Jeremy Hunt, called for a culture of openness where poor care never went unchallenged. Much less space and time was devoted, however, to finance and the influence of policy on issues. Little was really new.

Within my *Collected Essays*, several deal with health matters. The first, in two parts, is '*Middlemarch* and the Doctors', written as long ago as 1948 and 1950. George Eliot had the gifts of a historian, and this is one reason why historians willingly turn to her. She emphasised the importance of veracity and a return to sources. *Middlemarch* was set in the years 1829 to 1832, a time when there was no stability. Dr Lydgate takes to a small provincial town great schemes, which he has learnt in a wider world. His radicalism applies to medical reform. It tells a tale of disillusionment. His 'scientific conscience got into the debasing company of money obligation and selfish respect'. 'From the beginning, medical history, partially the history of ideas, had to be related to hospital history, largely the history of institutions.' Eliot was not alone in giving health reform a central place in her thoughts. 'I see one work to be done 'ere I die', Charles Kingsley wrote to a friend in 1857, 'Sanitary Reform'. In Middlemarch a new hospital was in the process of being built when Lydgate arrived. It was sponsored by Bulstrode, an evangelical banker.

I included that article in part 1 of the second volume of my essays called 'Poets and Novelists'. The next section was called 'Problems and Policies' and included two articles specifically on health and one on the welfare state in historical perspective. I quoted at the beginning of part 2 Humphry House's *The Dickens World* (1941). 'In *Pickwick* a bad smell was a bad smell: in *Our Mutual Friend* it is a problem.' Chadwick's approach to the world at the beginning of the nineteenth century was Benthamite. Before 1830 he had begun to study typhus in the rookeries of East London From the heart of the capital, as

Secretary of the Poor Law Commission, he urged the need for a great improvement in sanitary conditions in the town.

Reading my lecture again I find it remarkably comprehensive and interesting. Who thought of the title I gave to it, 'The Age of Chadwick'? The characters in the story of public (and private) health are often very interesting, particularly Lord Shaftesbury, then Ashley, who as an evangelical Christian explored the East End on foot in 1844, the year of the founding of the Health of Towns Association. Statistics could matter as much as religion. The culminating Public Health Act of 1848 satisfied neither radicals nor opponents of public health legislation. *The Times* favoured the Bill: 'If this bill will not do, what will?' I ended my lecture with a statement on the importance of public opinion, made by Lord Shaftesbury in 1848:

> We wish to beget . . . to create and to sustain a true, firm, paramount and wise public opinion . . . It is not by law, it is not by individual efforts, it is not by the desultory attempts of a few benevolent people [that improvement in public health could come, but by] a wise, benevolent and instructed public opinion.

My lecture on public opinion and public health was first delivered as a lecture in the New Art Gallery at Leicester as the thirty-seventh of the annual lecture series of the Gatwick Trust. It was subsequently published as a pamphlet by the Gatwick Trust.

My article on 'Cholera and Society in the Nineteenth Century' first appeared in *Past and Present* in 1961. Beginning with the world outbreaks of 'Asiatic cholera' during the nineteenth century, the first one striking Britain in 1831, the last of them in 1893, I traced the response to the disease in different countries. It was thought of, pre-eminently, as 'a disease of society'. Among the cities which I mentioned was Lyons, which figures in other chapters in this book.

Nursing could do little about cholera. It was nursing, however, that I was most concerned with in the busiest year of my life after Dick Crossman, who was Secretary of State for Health and Social Security, in the spring of 1970 asked me to chair a committee on nursing education. I willingly accepted his invitation because I wanted to do something really useful for the community (I had turned down industrial relations). He left the choice of the members of the committee to me. In our departmental terms of reference we were asked to 'review the role of the nurse and the midwife in the hospital and the community, and the education and training required for that role, so that the best use is made of available manpower to meet present needs and the needs of an integrated health service'. It was the last phrase in this remit which distinguished our enquiry from that of our predecessors. It was an advantage to Crossman and to me that I had no experience of nursing. When my committee first met, I told them to forget about any of the previous reports on nursing they had read. They were only too happy to concur.

I had an efficient civil servant as secretary, Elisabeth Singleton, but I did not allow her to have anything to do with the writing of the final report, which I did by myself. It was very well received by most nurses, although not by health visitors or to a certain extent by midwives. At the meetings of the committee, I had deliberately placed next to me the most conservative of all the matrons (Miss G. E. Watts). It was an advantage to me that she came from Leeds. I also had as my vice-chairman a Professor whom I came to trust and like, Ivor R. C. Batchelor from Edinburgh. Among the members of the committee was a very lively young nurse who in some ways contributed most, Miss Susan Pembrey. The most senior and helpful nurse was Miss Sheila Collins. The most interesting member was Elspeth Howe, wife of Geoffrey Howe, a Conservative statesman. She was the only recommendation by Crossman. We had two Advisors, Nicholas Bosanquet and Jillian MacGuire. In the course of our enquiries we collected evidence from a wide range of individuals and bodies, some solicited, others sent in to us. We also made our own research. We made visits to a large number of hospitals and educational institutes. I now find in writing *Loose Ends and Extras*, that in 1978 a graduate student, J. A. Birch, wrote a thesis on 'Anxiety in Nursing Education: With Particular Reference [to my report]'. It won him a doctorate at Newcastle.

In 1990 I gave the Osler Oration (a lecture in memory of the Canadian physician Sir William Osler) which was printed in the *Journal of the Royal College of Physicians*. In it I said that 'a historian must place Osler firmly within the context of his own time, although much that he had to say and to write about was thought by him as timeless'. He was, indeed, interested in time as well as in history and once, in 1891, he described the period in which he was living as 'the childhood of the world'. He was then in his own forties. He emphasized the need not only for skills but for strength of character and for broadness of outlook:

> A physician may possess the science of Harvey and the art of Sidenham and yet there may be lacking in him those finer qualities of heart and head which count for so much in life ... Medicine is seen at its best in men of ... the highest and most harmonious culture. Doctors have long been interested in history, both of the profession and of the places where it has been practised.

A key date in health history was 1949, the year of the opening to scholars of Sir Henry Wellcome's superb library. Wellcome, a great collector, was born six years after Osler and lived seventeen years longer. As a social historian I turn regularly to the *Bulletin of the Society for the Social History of Medicine*, founded in 1970, and for one year in its short life I had the honour to be its president. In 1970 it was accepted that the membership of the Society would be inter-disciplinary. The years between 1970 and 1980, like the years immediately preceding 1970, saw enormous changes not only in medicine but in the study of history as a discipline.

Chapter 6

The Great War:
Why Remember It and How?

It sometimes seems more difficult to forget than to remember. We consciously remember much in our public past. In our post-modern age the media make us as aware as they possibly can do of anniversaries, jubilees, centenaries, bicentenaries and tercentenaries. The last two of these are beyond human memory. The media now go back further in time to remind us of events which preceded the modern age. They are actively interested also in their own history.

There is nothing specifically twenty-first century in such media attention. I have before me as I begin this chapter an article of 1988 by Benjamin Woolley called 'The Anniversary Business' which posed the question 'What shall we commemorate this week?' The year 1988 was being defined almost entirely in terms of past years. The Australian bicentennial was only one. The Spanish Armada intruded as did the 'Glorious Revolution' of 1688.

In 2013 we celebrated the centenary of the Chelsea Flower Show, an annual event, organised by the Royal Horticultural Society, which itself dates back to 1804. In all our gardens we distinguish, as the Show does, between annuals and perennials and perhaps we should do so in all our historical remembrances. The Royal British Legion remembers the Great War of 1914 to 1918 annually by a wild flower, the red poppy, which grew in profusion on the battlefields in Picardy. It was growing there long before the British Legion, not then Royal, came into existence.

Each year a Festival of Remembrance is held not in the open air but in the Royal Albert Hall, and like the Cenotaph parades is televised by the BBC each year. It is a combination of camaraderie, spectacle and religious service. Among those performing in the 2013 Festival in the presence of the Queen were the Poppy Girls, five daughters of fathers now serving in the Forces around the world, chosen in a competition. They sang a Poppy Appeal single, *The Call*, 'No Need to Say Goodbye'. As always, the evening festival ended with a two-minute silence. That itself is perhaps the most evocative remembrance of Armistice Day 1918, whether it is held in the evening as at the Festival or in the morning as on Remembrance Sunday.

Breaking the silence or not wearing a poppy was a social crime in 2013. Journalists and broadcasters were as aware of this as were politicians. If they did not wear poppies, they were ostracised. The silence and poppy wearing were part of remembrance far from the Cenotaph, where members of the royal family were the first to lay wreaths of poppies, or in the Albert Hall where they were in abundant display. Poppies have become symbols of war everywhere.

On the very impressive Remembrance Day service in Whitehall in 2013 the royal family dominated the proceedings, and much was made of the fact that the Great War ceremonies to be held in 2014 would be even more impressive. The ceremony does not lose its wonder with the passing years and covers not only the Great War, of which there are now no survivors, but all the wars in which this country has been involved since. The 2013 service was held in brilliant autumn sunshine, and the intake of participants was stopped by the police when the site was judged to be full to capacity. No fewer than 10,000 people lined up and waited to march past the Queen. Politicians and religious leaders of various denominations laid their wreaths. The boom of a Great War field gun initiated the two minutes' silence in the heart of the capital. The 2013 parade took over an hour to pass the Cenotaph. It was led by the War Widows Association. A delegation from the British Korean Veterans Association joined the parade for the last time. That war, largely forgotten except in the American film and television series *M*A*S*H*, cost the lives of 1,339 British service personnel. It left Korea divided. 2013 was the last time that the Korean veterans will parade because most of the survivors of the war are now in their eighties. News from the strange regime in North Korea still comes through. It is nearly as horrifying as war itself.

The parade also included a loudly cheered group of Gurkhas who passed on the way a small group of protesting Gurkhas who had been mounting a vigil for the past fortnight in Whitehall at the foot of the statue of Viscount Montgomery. They had launched a hunger strike there as part of their campaign for better pensions, medical treatment, and settlement rights for Gurkha veterans and their families. They had found a dedicated English champion in Joanna Lumley.

While all this was going on in Whitehall, in Afghanistan Prince Andrew and the Defence Secretary laid their wreaths down at Camp Bastion, Helmand Province, where 446 British personnel had lost their lives since 2001. In continental Europe the Royal British Legion held a tribute at the Menin Gate in Ypres and planted a field of poppies there. The Duke of Edinburgh and Prime Minister David Cameron were both present. Cameron's great, great uncle had been killed at the Second Battle of Ypres in 1915.

Poppies figure in my personal life. When I was an undergraduate at Cambridge, going up a year before the beginning of the Second World War, 'Poppy Day' was a great annual event. When the number of undergraduates fell because many of them were called up in a war that was very different from the Great War I was chosen to run a war-time Poppy Day. As a 'reward' I dined at High Table in King's College, escorted arm-in-arm to the table by the venerable Provost. He had more than poppies on his mind.

I was born in 1921, only three years after what was called Armistice Day brought the Great War to its end, and one of my earliest memories is being carried on my father's shoulders to watch the inauguration of Keighley's War Memorial. It was sited, not on a long and broad boulevard like the Cenotaph in Whitehall, but confined in a square, the Town Hall Square, which kept its name. It was at the heart of the town, and opposite it was Keighley's public library, endowed by Andrew Carnegie. In 2013 I responded intuitively to the War Memorials Trust, a small charitable trust which asks us 'What can you do to look after your local war memorials?'

The Trust is not directly responsible for any war memorials and has no legal authority. It is a mistake, therefore, to compare it with the Imperial War Graves Commission, which owes a great deal to the efforts of one man, Fabian Ware, a largely forgotten character. He was a director of Rio Tinto when war was declared in 1914, and, at the age of forty-five, judged too old to join the British Army. He made his own way to France in September 1914 to command a mobile unit of the Red Cross in which he worked as an ambulance driver. As he moved around he observed that the graves of soldiers who had been killed were not being properly marked. On his initiative, and largely due to his efforts, a Graves Registration Commission was set up. Very soon it began answering enquiries from dead solders' relatives. The outcome was the Imperial War Graves Commission, established in May 1917. After the end of the war it employed distinguished architects, among them Sir Edward Lutyens, to design cemeteries and memorials.

Nevertheless, the Commission was not universally supported. It was called a tyranny, and even stronger language was used. The sculptor Eric Gill, whom I introduced into Chapter 4 for his sculptures outside Broadcasting House, called standardised headstones for the dead a 'Prussian imposition'. The support of Winston Churchill when he was Secretary of State for War was crucial. 'The Commission was discharging a high mission in seeking to give dead soldiers memorials that would last for hundreds of years.' Rudyard Kipling tried to offer Ware positive practical help. He suggested that 'Their Name Liveth for Evermore' from Ecclesiasticus should be inscribed on a Stone of Remembrance in each cemetery.

It was only during the Great War and after it that for the first time in history the names of soldiers of all ranks were inscribed for posterity on public war memorials in towns and villages across the country and in schools, universities and other institutions. I always look carefully at them. The number of people killed brings out more eloquently than words the sense of loss and of sacrifice.

It is more difficult to remember women who were not fighting in the Great War, but through their families were deeply involved in it. It is hard to do justice to it on television. Tamara Rojo, artistic director at the English National Ballet and one of its principal dancers, is preparing to star in a three-part series of ballets about the Great War called *Lest We Forget*. As the war went on, many women were involved in munitions production and other war efforts, thereby making a collective contribution to the war, which could not have been won without them.

How shall we remember the Great War? There are contrasting opinions. Some people object even to wearing poppies. The University of London Students Union took a decision effectively to bar its senior officers from taking part in the Cenotaph ceremony. A similar boycott was staged in 2012 when one of the Union's vice-presidents said that the Great War was a 'colonial scramble for possessions, markets and resources amongst the major nations'.

The Education Secretary, Michael Gove, had no sympathy with this approach. Writing in the *Daily Mail*, he said that school children should learn about the Great War 'in the right way', honouring the 'heroism and sacrifices of our great grandparents' and rejecting the supposedly left-wing view, propagated by fictional television pro-grammes such as *Blackadder*, that the war was a 'misbegotten shambles'. Sir Tony Robinson (Baldrick in *Blackadder*) took him on.

There were ambitious public plans to commemorate the war in more than 2,000 plays, performances and exhibitions. These were to continue over four years. Diane Lees, Director-General of the Imperial War Museum, a great institution which was brought into existence after the Great War, announced that as part of the celebrations the Museum would open new galleries costing £5 million. They would display weapons, uniforms, diaries, letters and 'souvenirs', alongside photographs, films and paintings, some of them never seen before. There was to be a First World War Centenary Partnership, a coalition of more than 1,800 museums, galleries, arts groups, tourist agencies, government bodies and some overseas organisations, to plan and implement a national programme.

Activities would necessarily involve centres outside London. Indeed, 'Around Britain' was an essential dimension. For example, there would be a flying display outside Highclere Castle, once known best for its connection with Tutankhamen and now for being Downton Abbey in the television series, and 'HMS – Hear My Story', an exhibition at the Museum of the Royal Navy in Portsmouth. Sadly that great shipbuilding city was in danger of being itself turned into a museum because the government was no longer providing funds to build ships.

Imperial War Museum North would stage the largest exhibition on the Great War in north-west England, 'From Street to Trench, a War that Shaped a Region'. Most interesting of all within the context of *Loose Ends and Extras* there was to be a new production of *Oh! What a Lovely War*, which would later make its way round the provinces.

Being aware of all this planning does not make it easier to answer the question posed in the title of this chapter – *Why* remember? The answer may seem obvious, but it is not. There are no people alive who fought in the Great War, and the number of people who lived through it diminishes each year. Memory is giving way to history, and historians have already made it clear that there are as many ways of interpreting this war as there are of interpreting all historical pro-cesses. There is no agreement on what are myths and what are facts. Are we celebrating in 2014 or trying to understand what happened?

There are contrary views of the Great War. Why should it be called great? Some talk of it in terms of triumph, others in terms of disaster. It depends only to a certain extent on vantage point. Are we as much interested in Germany, the wartime enemy and its allies, as we are in ourselves and our allies? As I write, all the disputed views of the Great War and what historians have said of it, sometimes passionately, have been openly raised. These start with disputes about its origins, which first interested me when I was an undergraduate

It is a gross over-simplification to assert flatly, as Boris Johnson has done, that Germany started the Great War. After the assassination of

Archduke Franz Ferdinand in Sarajevo Austria-Hungary was determined to start a war. Germany offered its support, and its diplomats felt that the war could be contained. Had Tsarist Russia refused to support Serbia there would only have been a Balkan war. Had France not backed Russia, to whom it was allied, there would have been no war. There is something to be said for the pre-war alliance system – at least in the way it operated – being the key to the start of the Great War. The United Kingdom, where the Liberal Cabinet was divided, did, I still maintain, join the war because of Belgium, and the German invasion of Belgium was real enough.

The German Schlieffen Plan, drawn up in 1905, involved their invading France through Belgium in order to bypass the heavily fortified Franco-German border. The Plan did not work. They did not go far enough west, as Schlieffen had urged, and could not surround Paris. There was an absurd situation in Paris itself in 1914. The city's military governor-general ordered demolition charges to be laid under the Eiffel Tower. The government was prepared to scuttle away to Bordeaux.

The Battle of the Marne which started on 4 September seemed to be going rather well at first for the French but within a few days the Germans had rallied. Great slaughter now began on both sides. The war turned into a protracted trench war stalemate that lasted for four years. The next year a campaign at Gallipoli, which Winston Churchill conceived of as a way of getting out of trench warfare, saw very heavy casualties. One of the officers fighting at Gallipoli was Clement Attlee, Churchill's Deputy Prime Minister in the Second World War. I once travelled on a cruise boat with him past the battle site. He told me that because he applauded Churchill's Great War strategy he was glad to be at his side in the Second World War. I was appalled by the heavy Australian casualties.

As far as the fighting is concerned I am not sure that there will be any more agreement either about how it was fought than about its 'causes'. To me not all of its generals were 'donkeys' leading 'lions'. When Alan Clark called them donkeys in 1961, his opinion was taken up by Joan Littlewood who had already decided to direct *Oh! What a*

Lovely War. She hated khaki and bemedalled generals, but insisted on the people who were writing the script going to talk to anybody who knew about the war, including soldiers and politicians who had been in power during the war.

Anthony Seldon, now Headmaster of Wellington School, has contested the view that public school alumni, who died at nearly twice the rate of other ranks in the Great War, were responsible both for taking Britain into the war and fighting the war in a way that showed shocking callousness towards rank and file soldiers. Believing that castigation of the public schools began in 1961 with the publication of Alan Clark's *The Donkeys*, Seldon thought that it was time for a fresh look. He has demonstrated that generals and junior officers were not for the most part callous in their attitudes to other ranks. The 'public school ethos', in Seldon's view, was not as sinister as it had been portrayed. Indeed, a public school education provided young officers with many qualities required to survive the horror of the trenches.

There can be no more measurable agreement about the consequences of the war than there were about its causes and its conduct. The last of these aspects takes us on to Versailles and John Maynard Keynes, who was present at the Versailles conference after the war had finished. Keynes wrote a best-seller, *The Economic Consequences of the Peace*, in which he castigated the politicians from different countries who wished to get as much in reparations for the war from Germany as they could. In other words the agreement at Versailles would ensure that the peace would not be a lasting one. It requires to be reviewed and this has been done admirably by Margaret MacMillan in her *Peacemakers: The Paris Conference of 1919 and Its Attempt to End War* (2001). Professor MacMillan, now Warden of St Anthony's College, is a Senior Fellow of Massey College, University of Toronto, whose first Warden, Robertson Davies, I introduced in Chapter 5.

Whether we are celebrating the Great War or wanting to understand it we have to rely on books and the reviews of books when we look back. There has never been a shortage of either, and as the centenary of the Great War years looms ahead their numbers multiply.

The best-seller of the year is Max Hastings's robust *Catastrophe: Europe Goes to War in 1914*, which *The Times* hailed rightly as 'at once moving, provocative and utterly engrossing'. Hastings has written massive and masterly best-selling volumes on the Second World War, but his book pushes the parallels between what I call the Great War and he calls the First World War and the Second World War too far. In doing so he raises as many questions as he answers. Some of them he dealt with skilfully and convincingly in a television programme which I watched. I am now largely dependent on television for my judgements on the Great War.

I myself was born between the two wars, which for me still seem very different from each other, and I have long feared that in the centuries ahead they will be telescoped together as if they were one. I recall with distaste some historians attached to labels talking of a Second Thirty Years War from 1914 to 1945. They left out of history 'small wars' – and there were many of these – and after 1945 the Cold War. They forget too that war can serve as a metaphor. It even figures in hymns, for example 'Onward Christian Soldiers, Marching Forth To War'.

Max Hastings, like Diane Lees, never refers to the Great War. Why it was called great fascinates me. A book which I found especially interesting when I read and reviewed it was Paul Fussell's *The Great War in Modern Memory*. He focuses on the horror of the war. There have been other extremely interesting books written about different facets of the Great War. In 1964, the fiftieth anniversary of the Great War, Herbert Read, knighted, wrote an article in the *Yorkshire Post* describing the Great War 'as a soldier saw it'. Read served with the Green Howards and was awarded the DSO and the MC. He began his article, 'Nature preserves our peace of mind by a merciful law that allows us in the course of time to forget our most dreadful experience, and remember only the trivial, the inconsequent and the pleasing.' Fear, horror, revulsion and revolt were immediate reactions to any particular event in the war. Dread persisted throughout. He meant by dread 'an unending awareness of doom, a feeling of being committed, to an unknown fate, and if they did not give way to despair, they became fatalistic or stoical. "What's the good of worrying? Pack up your troubles in your old kit-bag."'

In 1998, with no jubilee or centenary in mind, Niall Ferguson wrote his best-selling *The Pity of War*, a radical reassessment of how the world hurtled into catastrophe in 1914. When the statesmen who took Europe to war in 1914 came to write their memoirs, they agreed on one thing: the war had been inevitable: 'The result of such vast historical forces, that no human agency could have prevented it.' For Lloyd George in his memoirs, as Big Ben struck 'the most fateful hour' on 4 August, it 'echoed in our ears, like the hammer of destiny. I felt like a man standing on a planet that had been suddenly wrenched from its orbit.' Such highly rhetorical words horrified Read.

There were to be almost as many criticisms of wartime politicians in the 1920s – Lloyd George perhaps excluded – as there were even of wartime field marshals, particularly Douglas Haig, and generals. Siegfried Sassoon, with his fascinating military record, wrote *Memoirs of a Fox-Hunting Man* (1928) and two years later, *Memoirs of an Infantry Officer*. Much of the criticism took the form of novels, some of them written by wartime soldiers. Erich Maria Remarque's *All Quiet on the Western Front* was written by a German soldier. One of the most interesting critical books in Britain, however, was by a woman, Vera Brittain, who published her *Testament of Youth* in 1933. Born in 1893 into a middle-class family, Vera had broken convention by winning an exhibition to Somerville College, Oxford, in 1914. The death of one of her brother's closest friends, who was killed in December 1915, stunned Vera, who had become a VAD nurse.

With the centenary imminent I turn to new books more than old ones. Richard Overy reviewed pertinent recent books, the first of them Hastings's *Catastrophe*. 'Nearly 100 years on', he writes, 'we are still trying to understand the paranoia that led to the First World War.' He also reviewed Frank Furedi's *First World War: Still No End in Sight*. Furedi suggested that 'we are still suffering from the fallout of the loss of certainty and cultural self-belief that the war provoked'. Why is Overy as afraid of calling it the Great War as Max Hastings or Diane Lees?

The other two books being reviewed include one by an author who is not afraid. Saul David's *100 Days to Victory: How the Great War was Fought and Won*. A very different writer, Marc Bostridge, whose historical writings I greatly admire, particularly his biography of Florence Nightingale, involved in a quite different war in the Crimea, has written *The Fateful Year: England 1914*. It is a book more about the prelude to war rather than the war itself. He assembles and analyses an immense mass of primary material to undermine the myths of 1914. His is not just a familiar story of a year divided into two halves when seven months of peace gave way to more than four years of brutal conflict.

The country was stunned into the war of supreme sacrifices that, in the words of the Remembrance Sunday edition of the *Sunday Telegraph* in 2013, were 'sacrifices that must never be forgotten'. 'Must' is a strong verb. Can it be enforced? 'It is not only serving soldiers who need support', the leader went on, 'there are many veterans struggling to survive physical, psychological or financial hardships and we have a responsibility to help them. Fortunately support is being given by many organisations and individuals. Yet public forgetfulness is a constant risk.' So too is public ignorance. There is also a danger of being swayed by propaganda. 'The ultimate purpose of this war', H. G. Wells wrote in 1914, 'is propaganda, the destruction of certain beliefs and the creation of others. It is to this propaganda that reasonable men must address themselves.' In 1918 he was saying almost the opposite of what he said in 1914.

As we move further away in time from the Great War and the number of people who know about it diminishes we need other ways of learning besides books. For example, we can take commemorative tours to the battlefields of the Great War in France and Belgium, particularly the Ypres salient and the Somme, to dispel ignorance of both history and geography. The best of the tours do.

I decided in writing *Loose Ends and Extras* not to go on a conducted tour, but on the invitation of my older son, Daniel, travelled by car to the Somme with his wife Annabel, my wife Susan and Doris my helper. It was the first time that I had been abroad since I came out of hospital after my visit to Hong Kong in 2012. We got to France via the Channel Tunnel, which had not been there when I spent a lot of time in the Somme as a boy. In a very real way for me my voyage was one of rediscovery. Nevertheless, the Somme was the first part of France that I knew. I stayed in 1934 with a family of textile manu-facturers, the Cordonniers, who lived near Cambrai, scene of a Great War battle, when British tanks were first used en masse. Jacques, their son, became a close friend. He was at the *lycée* in Cambrai.

Ours was a most enlightened school exchange, family to family. We also got to know people and places. It was with Jacques that I had my first encounter with Great War battlefields, cemeteries and war memorials.

The Cordonniers had a summer villa in Ault on the Channel coast, which they rented or leased, and it was there that I planned for us to end our trip to the Somme. The nearest town was Le Tréport which had been designated by the War Graves Commission as the possible site of a Great War cemetery. In 2013 we stayed in Arras, which was a far more delightful town than I remembered it from 1934. I preferred Amiens then with its great Gothic cathedral, and I retained the cathedral in my memory. Another city which I retain in my memory was Lille, occupied by the Germans during the Great War. It was a smoky industrial city when I visited it three times before 1939. After the building of the high speed railway, also not available when I was a boy travelling from Keighley, I stayed in Lille long after the smoke had gone and it had become a city of culture.

Our visit to Ault was worth all the waiting for if only because we had the most delicious oysters there. Yet there was much in the Somme which I did not like, its ghastly buildings and most of the people we met who lived there did not seem to recognise that they were dependent on the Great War tourist trade. I qualified this judge-ment based on our visits when I listened to the BBC Radio 3 Sunday feature, *Somme*, a documentary written by a Liverpudlian poet, Paul Farley, who travelled the 152-mile course of the River Somme from its source to the sea. We heard the sound of his trudging boots against the trickling, in places rushing, sound of the river. It was all evocative, more evocative than we had found it. For me there was a personal dimension to the programme, which did not leave out the fog and the mustard and chlorine gas in the last great German offensive of March 1918.

Farley had written another documentary, *Crossing the Bay*, which I heard last year. It was about Morecambe Bay, which Jacques Cordonnier and I saw in the last months of peace before the Second World War. A final irony. Apparently the name Somme derives from a Celtic word meaning tranquillity.

The relationship between film, fiction, fact and legend has always interested me. It was impossible to broadcast voices from the trenches. In any case those men who had been fighting in them did not like to talk about the horrors they had experienced. They preferred singing war songs, some of them bawdy, some of them about trench life, to talking about their day-to-day experiences. Under strict military orders they were not allowed to take snapshots or photographs. Surprisingly, Andrew Davidson, writing in the *Sunday Telegraph*, has found three battered photograph albums kept by his grandfather who died two days before he was born. He was a young doctor working with the Cameronians and had illicitly smuggled a folding camera into France and had taken informal pictures of his colleagues.

Even more surprisingly one of the albums consisted of photographs taken by another young Cameronian medical lieutenant. Sadly the albums stop in April 1915 when his grandfather, who won the Military Cross, was shot in the hip and hand while treating a casualty in no-man's land and very nearly died. We have far more visual and documentary evidence about the Great War than I ever expected to find.

In 1990, again not a jubilee or centenary year of the Great War, Sam Hynes, a Princeton professor, had published a book *A War Imagined*. In it he set out to discuss why the grip of the Great War should be so enduring and why the mythology of that cataclysm initially took shape. Like Read, he wrote about war having himself come through the fire. He was a US combat pilot in the Second World War. He describes how the ghastly tale of idealistic young men shipped to the slaughterhouse by their criminally stupid elders generated in British society 'a sense of radical discontinuity'.

Interested in art, as many journalists writing about the centenary are, he did not go into great detail about individual artists. For the journalists of 2013–14 there was one very special artist to remember. Stanley Spencer is even described by one of them as being the Giotto of England. An exhibition of his Great War paintings was staged in the autumn of 2013. It drew on Spencer's experiences as an orderly in the Royal Army Medical Corps at hospitals in Bristol and Macedonia. Normally Stanley Spencer's paintings shown then at Somerset House are at the Sandham Memorial Chapel at Burghclere in Hampshire. The exhibition was described as a once-in-a-lifetime event. 'To see them as they are displayed and lit in London is to see them as they have never been seen before.' The series begins with a painting showing a convoy of shell-shocked soldiers arriving at the gates of the Beaufort Hospital, Bristol.

What of the paintings of German and Austrian artists? Should we be remembering them? An exhibition is planned to show the work of German artists, among them Ernst Ludwig Kirchner whose works include a picture called 'Self Portrait as Soldier'.

There is a different exhibition at the National Portrait Gallery. It reveals the diversity of war portraiture. As well as writers, Charles Masterman's Propaganda Bureau also employed artists under an Official War Artists Programme. One of the painters was William Orpen. His Field Marshal Haig is a cool and calm Commander-in-Chief. His anonymous Grenadier Guardsman presents an ideal soldier. More exciting is Godfrey Malins's documentary film *The Battle of the Somme* which may be compared with its German counterpart, *With Our Heroes on the Somme*. There is scope for a separate exhibition of war posters. They cover every kind of propaganda.

Poets provide vivid depictions of the Great War even more than painters. Rupert Brooke and Wilfred Owen, often compared, are not the only two who deserve to be remembered. Siegfried Sassoon wrote some wonderful poems, one of them 'To Any Dead Officer' which has the savage last line, 'I wish they'd killed you in a decent show'. He no longer believed that the Great War was 'a decent' show, not because he was sympathetic in any way to pacifist critics of the Great War, of whom there were many and several whom he knew, usually called 'conchies', in other words they were conscientiously objecting to war. Charles Hamilton Sorley, a public-school man, son of a professor and cited by Anthony Seldon, joined the army in late September 1914 and settled down reluctantly to life as a soldier expecting the war to last three years and end in 'stalemate'. His most famous war poem was 'When You See Millions of the Mouthless Dead'. This was about the finality of death. It was found in his kit-bag after his death in October 1915 in the Loos offensive. He had been shot in the head by a sniper's bullet. He was twenty years old.

Wilfrid Owen, who won the Military Cross in 1918, wrote a number of still widely read poems including 'Anthem for Doomed Youth' which described 'bugles calling for them from sad shires'. He also wrote 'Dulce et Decorum Est' and 'Futility' and a poem greatly admired by Robert Graves, 'Disabled', about a man who lost his legs and an arm in action and was now back from the conflict and felt the camaraderie was 'stronger than any hatred of Germans'.

Isaac Rosenberg, a private in the 12th Suffolk Regiment, a 'bantam battalion' for men under 5 feet 3 inches tall, repudiated patriotism and wrote what has been judged the best poem of the war, 'Break of Day in the Trenches'. It tells the story of a rat that jumped over the poet's hand one morning in the Western Front.

> Droll rat, they would shoot you if they knew
> Your cosmopolitan sympathies.
> Now you have touched this English hand
> You will do the same to a German.

Rosenberg was killed near Arras, aged twenty-seven, in the major German offensive of April 1918. Owen was killed only four days before the armistice, having been wounded and returned to England and sent back to the trenches again having been declared fit.

There was a musical contribution to the war also. In 1917 Ralph Vaughan Williams wrote a pastoral symphony inspired not by British meadows at home, but by the starkly bleak battlefields of northern France. Vaughan Williams was serving as a stretcher bearer and ambulance driver.

There is only one happy Anglo-German event to note during the war. On Christmas Day 1914 British, French and German soldiers on the Western Front stopped shooting to sing carols and play football. Such fraternisation would not be repeated in the ensuing three Christmases. War went on.

The reminiscence of this incident, which was never typical of trench warfare, should not be the only wartime reminiscence of sport. On a chilly day this year, 23 March, a group of soccer players, managers and administrators, including Greg Dyke, head of the Football Association, gathered in France to commemorate professional soccer's only recipient of the Victoria Cross, Donald Bell. They brought his medal to his grave. It had never been out of England before. The event had a personal significance for me. Bell played for Bradford Park Avenue, the team I used to watch as a boy. No one then would have predicted either that the club would cease to exist or that the Borough of Keighley would be incorporated into the City of Bradford.

I have learnt many things about sport and the Great War in writing this book. Early in the Battle of the Somme Bell won his VC. Later in that terrifying battle, the oldest victim of the over-the-top horrors was Henry Walker, sixty-seven years old when with difficulty he enlisted. He had been a talented cricketer and captain of the Gatwick Golf Club. Not everyone who gave his life belonged to the ranks of Wilfred Owen's 'doomed youth'. I have learnt an immense amount, more than I could ever have expected, about 'ordinary soldiers' in the Great War, one of them an uncle of mine who was killed. We have heard the lost voices from the trenches which were thought to be too harrowing to be broadcast when the BBC collected them in 1964. One of them describes bayonetting an enemy, while others dwelt on the shelling, artillery bombardments so intense that they lost their self-control.

Hearing their voices encouraged me to listen to the voices not of combatants but of survivors. I could talk to them. One was a poet, Edmund Blunden, born in 1896. He lived on until 1974 and I got to know him. not in Suffolk where he moved in his last years, but in Hong Kong where he worked for a time. Surviving the war was the easy part, he wrote. Nightmares were a feature of his long post-war experience. He had fought at Passchendaele, Ypres and the Somme. He published a prose memoir, *Undertones of War*, in 1928. My favourite poem of his was 'Third Ypres'. In the madness of battle he watched a family of around twenty field mice. They calmed him down. 'On them depended my salvation.'

I have in my own possession an *Officer's Manual of the Western Front*, a compilation of facsimile reproductions of chapters and extracts from various army manuals in use during the Great War. The editor, Stephen Bull, writes that 'the Great War of 1914 is frequently described as bloody, stupid and simple. Bloody it undeniably was. Almost no family in Britain was untouched. In certain respects it was stupid too. Some have suggested that the United Kingdom should never have entered the conflict. Others that it was vain sacrifice.' According to Bull the war was never simple, however. 'Once started the struggle between prosperous and populous nations, endowed with industrial strength and great technological virtuosity, could not remain uncomplicated for long.'

Perhaps I should end there. Instead, having introduced Rosenberg's rat, I should mention another animal, the horse. More horses were involved in the Great War than in any other war that Britain fought. The cavalry horses were the most famous, but workaday animals kept troops moving. In 2011 a film was made called *War Horse* which paid a moving tribute to the horses in the war and to one horse in particular, the horse that belonged to a young boy. The film was based on a children's novel by Michael Morpurgo, written in 1985. A play *War Horse*, which started at the National Theatre is still showing in the West End and around the provinces.

Chapter 7

Words, Links, Coincidences

I began the first chapter of the third volume, *The War of Words*, of my *History of Broadcasting in the United Kingdom*, published in 1970: 'Words do not win wars. Nonetheless, between 1939 and 1945 there was a prolonged war of words which has sometimes been thought of less flatteringly as wordy warfare in which the BBC took a leading part.' These far from wordy words provide an excellent link with my last chapter on the Great War.

I called the first chapter of my 1970 volume 'Perspectives', and the main point I made, in what in effect was a preface, was that the existence of broadcasting constituted the main difference in propaganda between the Great War and the Second World War. I was interested in propaganda long before 1970. My interest grew when I served in the Intelligence Corps as a code-breaker at Bletchley Park. We had near neighbours in Woburn Abbey where there was not only a WAAF (Women's Auxiliary Air Force) outpost of the Park but also in the house itself a group of people working on propaganda to our war enemies.

Because of the Official Secrets Act I was not allowed in 1970 to refer specifically to the wartime operations at Bletchley Park or Woburn Abbey. Nor in the biographic blurb on the dust cover of *The War of Words* was it stated that I had served in the Intelligence Corps during the Second World War. There were hidden secrets in my wartime life which I could not disclose even to my wife. She did know that I had been serving at Bletchley Park, but did not know what I had been doing there. Together we had been to Woburn Abbey as guests of Lord and Lady Tavistock, but we were mainly interested in the appearance and contents of the Abbey and in the controversial life story of the Duke of Bedford, the owner of the Abbey. I did not feel that Susan or any of the guests was interested in what was going on at the Abbey in wartime.

I myself did not know much about pre-BBC propaganda in the Great War. Eventually I was to read about it in detail in a book published in 1985, *The Great War of Words*, subtitled *Literature as Propaganda 1914–18 and After*. It was written by Peter Buitenhuis, a Professor of English at Simon Fraser University in British Columbia, Canada, a new university like Sussex, which I visited twice before 1985 because it was new. Buitenhuis had an interesting older story to tell. In the afternoon of 2 September 1914 twenty-five of Britain's most famous authors gathered around a great blue conference table in Wellington House in Buckingham Gate, London. This was the home of the National Health Insurance Commission. Why there? C. F. G. Masterman, a Liberal Cabinet minister whom I always think of simply as Charles Masterman, had published a book which I read as an undergraduate and which I have often re-read, *The Condition of England*, and he had been appointed Minister of Propaganda by Asquith when war was declared on the Kaiser's Germany. There is an unusual link there, and there is also a coincidence. I taught a Masterman descendant (grandson?) when I was a tutor at Worcester College after the Second World War.

The authors sitting round the table in 1914 were among the most influential authors in Britain. The only two important writers who were not present were Bernard Shaw and Bertrand Russell. Among the twenty-five there were Thomas Hardy, the Poet Laureate Robert Bridges, Arnold Bennett, G. K. Chesterton, Sir James Barrie, Sir Arthur Conan Doyle, John Galsworthy, Hall Caine, John Masefield, Henry Newbolt, who was popularly known for his patriotic and imperialist poems but was also a naval historian, the Professor of Poetry in Oxford from 1906–11, J. W. Mackail, and William Archer, the best-known London drama critic of the period and the man most responsible for introducing Ibsen to British audiences.

It is possible to say interesting and relevant things about each of these writers. They carried with them ample baggage. Hardy was nearing the end of his life and his melancholy poetry still attracts readers more than the ambitious poem 'The Dynasts'. Bridges was to be much taken up by the BBC after it was founded in 1922. Bennett, who was to be very closely associated with the Ministry of Propaganda, was a much-read novelist who disagreed in public about the purposes of novels, arguing with Henry James. James, having lived in England for nearly forty years, judged that with the outbreak of war 'civilisation had been plunged an abyss of blood and darkness'. Barrie was the creator of Peter Pan, who still lives, never to grow up. Conan Doyle scarcely needs to be described. He had killed off Sherlock Holmes but was forced to bring him back to life. Galsworthy was a very influential playwright who dealt with still topical problems concerning truth, justice and equality. He was perhaps best known for his *Forsyte Saga*, which was a great success when broadcast as a television series. Caine was probably the most popular novelist of his time and was a member of other important national committees. John Masefield bid us all to 'go down to the sea tonight', and Henry Newbolt had written what is probably the most famous poem about cricket – 'There's a breathless hush in the close tonight / Ten to make and the match to win.' The Great War was never a game, and the famous game of football played between the Allied and German trenches at Christmas 1914 was 'one of a kind', never to be repeated.

Religion figured quite prominently on the list of invited writers. A. C. Benson was a famous Eton master, novelist, critic and bio-grapher of his father the Archbishop of Canterbury. R. H. Benson another son of the Archbishop, became a noted Catholic author and a monsignor as well as a novelist, Israel Zangwill was a well-known Zionist, a journalist and dramatist. These writers were to be employed in diverse ways during the war.

An article by S. K. Ratcliffe, 'The English Intellectuals in War-time' (I would query the naming of them as intellectuals, a word far less used in Britain than in continental Europe) pointed out that in 1914 'few could have foreseen how literary craftsmen could have been drawn into the public service as translators, censors and pamphleteers in the Foreign Office, the Press Bureau and the propaganda agencies'. What he said was true. Some of the people employed as pamphleteers were given uniforms, among them John Buchan, who years later was to become Governor-General of Canada and given the title Lord Tweedsmuir, and John Masefield who was uniformed in the Royal Navy.

Masefield gave a false account of what had happened and was happening at Gallipoli. Buchan, author of some fine novels, among them *The Thirty-Nine Steps*, was employed to describe the fighting in the Battle of the Somme. He produced an account which left out all the horror of it. He praised the generals and the troops who were sent over the top as 'the splendid troops who shed their blood like water for the liberty of the world'. They were always 'bronzed'. In fact 1 July 1916, when the Battle of the Somme began, was the blackest day in the history of the British Army. Of about 110,000 men who made the assault 57,540 were casualties, 20,000 of them killed. The German Army had only 8,000 casualties. Buchan claimed that the German losses were far higher. At the end of that day Buchan was having dinner with the generals on the Somme and wrote to his wife 'A perfect summer day and larks are singing above the bombardment.'

The first aim of the Ministry of Propaganda was to secure American support. There was a small but not insignificant German-speaking element in the United States, some of them immigrants, more of them the children of the previous generation of German immigrants. They were very strong in Wisconsin. They were associated there with beer more than with politics. After the United States joined the war on Germany, it was clear that German voices in the United States would be largely silenced.

In the last stages of the Great War there were significant changes in politics in Britain. The fall of the Asquith government in December 1916 was a very sharp break. It was inevitable that Masterman would now be demoted and indeed he lost his place in the organisation of propaganda. Buchan was appointed Director of a new Department of Information, but moved from the centre of the scene in favour of Max Aitken, soon to be Lord Beaverbrook. Beaverbrook had been horrified by the slaughter on the Somme, as had been David Lloyd George, who took Asquith's place as Prime Minister. Beaverbrook became Minister of Information in 1917 with Arnold Bennett, who was Director of Propaganda in France, at his side. Beaverbrook wrote by far the best book on the politics of the war, *Politicians and the War*, published in two volumes in 1928 and 1932.

There were important links between the organisation and role of the Ministries of Information and wartime propaganda of the Great War and the Second World War. BBC broadcasts in German began during the Czech crisis of September 1938. They took a new turn in March 1939 after the fall of Prague. News bulletins called *Sonderberichter* were now subject to fewer restraints than had been imposed upon the BBC by Sir Campbell Stuart, a veteran of Crewe House, the propaganda centre at the end of the Great War. In 1920 Hodder and Stoughton had published his *Secrets of Crewe House*. Campbell Stuart operated from 1 September 1939 from Electra House. In 1940 it was planned to transfer his Enemy Propaganda Unit to the Foreign Office. Campbell Stuart was less happy working with Churchill's Coalition Government than he had been with Neville Chamberlain's Conservative Government and disappeared from the scene.

The subsequent history of BBC propaganda is too complicated to tell even briefly here. I have described it fully in *The War of Words*. I trace the relationship between the Ministry of Information, the Foreign Office, and the Political Warfare Executive, another threesome, and also look at the new characters involved in the story. By a coincidence I discovered a cartoon of Reith called 'A Sop to Cerberus or the Dog's Chance'. I have raised Cerberus in a completely different Oxford connection in the first chapter of this book.

Cartoons connect different themes and different periods in history. We always have to look at the words in them as well as the images. In a book by John Wells, *Rude Words: A Discursive History of the London Library*, published in 1991, the year I left Oxford, the manuscript of which he asked me to read, he goes back to Thomas Carlyle to trace the origins of the library and to the lectures that Carlyle gave in the campaign to raise funds to open it. One of Carlyle's lectures was given in the Freemasons' Tavern which has all kinds of connections with radicalism, secularism, Chartism and socialism. Some of them were given in Portman Square; by a coincidence, when I was President the Workers Educational Association (WEA) had its headquarters there. The building is now a hotel. The lectures Carlyle gave on 'Heroes and Hero Worship' attracted a large fashionable audience One of the people listening to him, James Spedding, saw the conflict between the steam locomotive and the philosopher's stone as lying behind what Carlyle had to say. He was proclaiming a new faith that would somehow reconcile the modern world in ancient awe steam power with roaring Jesus sulphur pools and volcanic chasms.

Carlyle wanted to support a new library, which would be open to all readers and allow them to borrow books. It was books that mattered most to him. He believed that among the most important books were biographies, for history consisted of multiple biographies. Each biography had wide-ranging ramifications.

In this respect I have looked carefully at the biographical inform-ation available about a man who has influenced my own life both as a thinker and as a writer, R. H. Tawney. Tawney, my great predecessor as President of the WEA, was born in Calcutta, a city that I know well and with which I have had many links. I remember one of the longest telephone calls in my life (the other long one was with Reith when he told me he was planning to destroy his diary) with Margaret Metcalf, who was trying to save the unlit Art Gallery there from destruction. Tawney spent most of his early childhood in Weybridge, Surrey, in a house near the river which he loved and which he fished from with his sister. He went on to Rugby School where William Temple, a future Archbishop of York and of Canterbury, was his contemporary. From Rugby he moved on to Balliol, Oxford, as a Scholar. In 1903 he got a Second in Greats. 'How do you propose to wipe out this disgrace?' his father asked him. Frank Fletcher, who had taught him Latin and Greek at Rugby, described Greats as the best examination in either Oxford or Cambridge, 'whatever class a man may be awarded in it'. Did that answer his father's question?

Tawney's first academic post was a humble one. Was that the answer? In 1906 Professor William Smart, a member of the Royal Commission on the Poor Law, asked Tawney to assist Tom Jones, a future Secretary to a succession of Prime Ministers, in the teaching of economics, not a part of Greats, in the University of Glasgow. His annual salary was worse than humble, £50, less than £1 a week. He sought to augment his income by writing for a newspaper first in Glasgow, then in London. Fabian Ware, a most interesting link, was then editor of the *Morning Post* and invited Tawney to write articles and leaders. They were necessarily ephemeral, and although I am President of the Ephemera Society I have not read any of them.

In 1905 Tawney became a member of the Executive Committee of the WEA, founded two years earlier by Albert Mansbridge, and in 1908 he was appointed to a pioneer post teaching tutorial classes under the aegis of Oxford University. The classes were not in Oxford but in Glasgow, Longton in the Potteries and Rochdale, home of the famous Co-operative pioneers. In Rochdale one of the members of the tutorial class was A. P. Wadsworth, future editor of the *Manchester Guardian*. We have already been in his office there! Tawney, who in 1909 had married a sister of William Beveridge, moved south again in 1913 to become Director of the Rattan Tata Foundation for the Study of Poverty in the London School of Economics where Beveridge was to become Director. After the Great War he moved to a Readership in Economic History at the LSE, holding it until 1931. Later he was to become a Professor of Economic History in the University of London.

During the Great War he had served in the ranks in the Manchester Regiment. This was completely in character. What was not was that he wrote and published articles about it, 'The Attack' appeared in the *Westminster Gazette* in 1916. A second article 'Some Reflections of a Soldier' appeared in the *Nation* and a third 'The Sword and the Spirit' in the *Athenaeum* in 1917. During the Second World War he was to serve briefly as Labour Attaché in Washington. He had favoured rearmament during the 1930s and wrote a powerful article for the *New*

York Times, 'Why Britain Fights'. He knew from personal experience what the differences between the Great War and the Second World War were.

Between the wars was his golden age as a historian and as a Labour publicist. His best-read book, *Religion and the Rise of Capitalism*, appeared in 1926, based on Scott Holland Lectures that he had given four years earlier. The book was rejected by the first publisher to whom he offered it. Within a year of its appearance under a different publisher its sales ran into six figures. It was to be one of the first Penguins after the war. When the Tawneys travelled to Australia in 1955, his first visit there – they had already been to China in 1931 – Professor Crawford at Melbourne University told Tawney that his books were probably more read in the university than in any other university in the world and that *Religion and the Rise of Capitalism* was familiar to children in the highest forms of Melbourne's secondary schools.

When Susan and I went to Australia nearly five years later I was highly critical of Professor Crawford's university curriculum. It focused far more on Italy and Tudor England than on Australia. When we were there I worked in the city's magnificent public library, preparing a chapter on Melbourne to include in my *Victorian Cities*, the only city in the Commonwealth to figure in it. I know that my chapter was influential in inspiring Australian historians to devote more attention to their own cities.

When we went out to Australia I was already very interested in words and had been since the war when I wrote an article on military slang. It was rejected by George Orwell, then editor of *Tribune* and I have never published it since. I followed the further development in military slang as the war went on and at the end of the war greatly extended my interest in words to cover words and indeed vocabularies of all kinds and was delighted that John Wells called his history of the London Library *Rude Words*. They interested me. An article that particularly engaged me was written by an American, A. E. Bestor, 'The Evolution of the Socialist Vocabulary' in the *Journal of the History of Ideas* in 1948. I note that in his invaluable book *Keywords* (1976), Raymond Williams also referred to the Bestor article.

My interest in words, their history and their usage, an interesting word in itself, goes back long before Raymond Williams, born in the same year as myself – three months after me! – and educated in Abergavenny Grammar School and Trinity College, Cambridge, published his fascinating book *Keywords: A Vocabulary of Culture and Society*. He had written an important book which I reviewed, *Culture and Society*, in 1958. That was my way of approaching words also. I knew Raymond as an adult education tutor for the Oxford University Delegacy for Extra-Mural Studies. I was a Delegate before I married and moved from Oxford to Leeds in 1955. In 1961, the year I arrived in Sussex University, he was elected a Fellow of Jesus College, Cambridge. Was this a coincidence? Our lives had moved in parallel. Sadly, however, his life was not as long as mine. He died in 1988.

In his writing Raymond Williams never mentioned Ivor Brown, who in a sense introduced me to the serious use of words in *Chosen Words* which came out as a Penguin in 1962. Our two lives have not moved in parallel. He was much older than Raymond and I. Born in Penang in 1890, from 1929 to 1954 he was closely connected with the *Observer* and that was how I came to know his work. *Chosen Words* consisted of studies which he called word-anthologies. It was a series which began as a single random wartime volume and had extended to eight, 'due largely', he said, to 'the good will of my readers who also became, in a way, my writers'. He was not approaching words through culture. However, he had long linguistic purposes. He referred in his Preface to the 'campaign against the verbal pomposities and poly-syllabic compositions of Officialese and Business English'. The government, he noted, through the 'excellent labours of Sir Ernest Gowers' had tried both to end the offences of civil servants and to improve the usage of English everywhere. In a handy and concise book called *The Complete Plain Words* containing in revised form his *Plain Words* and *The ABC of Plain Words*, Brown was offering what was called 'an admirable cheap guide to the Queen's English'.

I originally intended to call this chapter 'Links, Connections and Coincidences'. I have therefore decided to say something in the chapter about connections though I have discarded the term from the title. As I said in my first chapter and indeed throughout this book, all things connect. I am interested in the fact that the Commonwealth of Learning (COL) calls its news bulletin *Connections*. Its July 2013 number commemorated the silver jubilee of COL, which has attempted since it started to bring together academics, civil servants and politicians. Among the messages of congratulation the one that COL received from the deputy vice-chancellor of the National University of Samoa struck a perfect note. 'This is really our celebration also,' he said, 'because we feel we have been very much a part of COL.'

I sent my own special greetings, for COL was founded on the initiative of Sonny Ramphal, then Secretary-General of the Commonwealth. He was an outstanding Secretary-General, full of ideas, with the determination to implement them. He asked me to write a report on what some people hoped would be a new international open university, but instead I recommended in my report a less academic and more practically orientated institution which would draw on the initiatives and contributions of people in different Commonwealth countries. Our proposals were set out in a 'Memorandum of Understanding' which was agreed upon by member countries in 1988. I remember that one of my most difficult tasks in securing Canadian agreement was to win the support of French-speaking Canada. I must have been persuasive. COL was to have its headquarters in Vancouver.

The July 2013 number has a middle section called 'In Focus' describing the work of COL through the years, dividing it into five categories – teacher education, open school, higher education, basic trade courses, and maternal and child health. It also noted the role of different personalities involved in its activities. Its founding President was Professor James A. Maraj, a Trinidadian of Indian origin – and a good cricketer. This number of *Connections* goes on to list all the subsequent presidents and the part that they have played in the development of COL.

It is difficult to write the history of culture without introducing many 'c' words, including communications. Coincidences close this chapter. There were coincidences in the life of John Logie Baird, who carried out the first demonstration of television in Hastings. The Chairman of Odhams, my publisher, wrote to Baird on the eve of his first demonstration, wishing him well. John Reith's wife was an Odhams. Gordon Selfridge, who figured prominently in what I wrote about retailing in 'Abiding Historical Interests', arranged for Baird to do a demonstration in London in his great store. Baird died in Bexhill, not very far from Hastings. There are links as well as coincidences there.

Only now in writing *Loose Ends and Extras* have I become fully aware of the intricacies of the communications revolution, the title of one of the Mansbridge lectures that I delivered in Leeds University in 1956, soon after I arrived there. I believe that I invented the term 'communications revolution'. Only now have I recalled that it was the *third* Mansbridge Lecture. I was not aware in 1956 that I was thinking in threes. In my Leeds lecture I pointed to the conjunctions of the year 1896 which I was to draw on later in books, even in textbooks. It was the year when Alfred Harmsworth founded the *Daily Mail*, when the first regular cinema show was presented in London's Leicester Square, when the first motor show was held in England and Marconi arrived in London with his bundle of wireless patents.

Given the number of new things happening in 1896 it is fascinating to move on a hundred years and turn to the year 1996. This was not only the centenary of Alexander Graham Bell's telephone but the sixtieth anniversary of the first regular BBC television service and the fiftieth anniversary of its resumption after the Second World War. Baird had lost the contest for which television system should be adopted for the running of a regular service; the question was should it be mechanical or electronic. His mechanical system had no chance of winning the trial in 1936. The electronic system was designed by a team of researchers working for EMI, Electrical and Musical Industries Ltd, created in 1931 by a merger of two gramophone companies. EMI was the first company in Britain to produce cathode ray tubes, essential for successful television.

Are these really coincidences in the way that we usually refer to the term? Or was it merely that developments coincided? It is when we turn to personal coincidences that an element of chance or luck enters the terminology. One coincidence that I remember in my own was a double one. When I was Provost of Worcester one of my closest colleagues was Francis Reynolds, a distinguished lawyer, who was also Chairman of Common Room. I knew both him and his wife, Susan, who was a music teacher. When my wife Susan and I were in Hong Kong at the end of 2011 for the Centenary of the University, we found that Francis and Susan and Susan and I (different Susans!) were staying in the same hotel. This was called the Meridien Cyberport Hotel and none of us had stayed there before. There was no sign of any cyber activity nearby. There has been a further coincidence, in this case involving two of us only. On an unpremeditated visit to New Zealand I was walking through a backstreet in Christ Church when I bumped into Susan Reynolds. Neither of us knew the other was in the country.

My wife was a girl when I, twelve years older, was guarding the Town Hall in Trowbridge, the town nearest to her own village home. When she was at school at Shaftesbury Convent, she was a friend of Judith White, a daughter of R. J. White, whose seminar I had attended when studying my Special Subject in Cambridge. White's seminar on Bentham and Coleridge has influenced my subsequent work as a historian in countless different ways. She was staying with the Whites in Sheringham. I do not know what happened to R. J. in the years after my seminar came to an end. Susan occasionally sees Judith.

I have found in talking to my daughter-in-law Annabel, Daniel's wife, that they had coincidences of an interesting kind in their own lives. They were travelling around a dangerous part of Turkey at the same time in two separate tours. They did not meet each other then. Nor did they meet when Annabel was a student at Nottingham University and one day found herself writing an essay on coincidences. When they did meet at Wimbledon and married and came to live near us in Lewes they were great friends with two other Briggses and were able to compare their different experiences.

There is one final coincidence that should end this chapter. 'The Homestead', not a very common name for a house, although doubtless more common than 'The Caprons' where I live, was the name of the house where Muriel Odhams lived in Sussex before she married John Reith. That was also the name of the house where Seebohm Rowntree lived and where I used to stay with his son and his wife when writing about him. He was the subject of one of my books.

I end this chapter with words. I am deeply interested in new words. In 1989, a landmark year in Europe's history, when the Berlin Wall came down and the Soviet Union was dissolved – some writers have called it the end of the century – John Ayto edited the *Longman Register of New Words*. Longman was the original publisher of Dr Johnson's *Dictionary* in 1755 and Roget's *Thesaurus* in 1852. Many of the words and phrases in Ayto's *Register* are no longer in use, I like 'no frills' which is.

I have kept a large number of press cuttings dealing with words some of which are worth picking out. One is called 'A Word for Everything' and begins 'If there is one book that is in most houses, perhaps even more often than the Bible, it is a dictionary. Dictionaries of all kinds sell in millions, and since the language is always changing, of the making of new ones there is no end.' One of my favourites is *The Oxford Dictionary of Proverbs*, edited by J. A. Simpson. It was reviewed by Auberon Waugh who found it extremely useful in tracing the origins of proverbs.

> Simpson offers readers Isaac Watts's 'Birds in their little nests agree', as if it were a piece of traditional wisdom rather than an obvious untruth coined by a clergyman at a desperate moment. Anybody who has seen young rooks – or other birds for that matter – in a nest will know that during their waking moments they are in a state of perpetual conflict.

Some readers might be mildly irritated, Waugh added, to learn that 'power corrupts' is now seen as a proverb, but they would find comfort in the discovery that Anthony Trollope thought of it exactly a year before Lord Acton.

Simpson had been chief editor of the *Oxford English Dictionary* before writing the *Oxford Dictionary of Proverbs*. He had succeeded

Robert Burchfield, whom I knew in Oxford and to whom Susan and I occasionally used to offer examples of new words that we had found and felt should be put into the dictionary. One of my favourite such words was 'phone-hacking'. Simpson, who had read English Literature at York and Medieval Studies at Reading, was appointed by Burchfield as his assistant at the *OED* and became chief editor in 1993, only the seventh since James Murray's appointment in 1879. Under Simpson's editorship more than 60,000 new words and meanings have been added to the *OED*.

The last of my press cuttings, which takes me back to a point in my own life which I have mentioned earlier in this chapter, appeared in *The Times* in an article written by Philip Howard called 'Mysteries of Oxford slang'. Howard knew as much about words as Ivor Brown. And in this interesting article he describes slang as being the most subjective register of language. 'It is the part of English that we feel most strongly that we have the right to lay down the law about, because we each make up and adapt our own slangs.' He refers to Oxford in his title because it was there that the '-ers' ending to words developed in the nineteenth century when the Radcliffe Camera came to be called the Radder and Jesus College Jaggers. Why Worcester college, which he describes as 'alma mater of all eminent jurors', became Wuggins was another matter beyond the scope of his enquiry. I do not know why myself.

Chapter 8

Pasts, Present, Futures

Before I had written a word of *Loose Ends and Extras* I had already been thinking about the shape, content and title of my first and last chapters. It seemed obvious to me then that I should call the first chapter 'Why This Book?', the same title as that which I had chosen for the first chapter of *Special Relationships: People and Places*. There was ample choice, however, in deciding what to call this last chapter. I thought first that I would call it 'The Big Picture', placing as much emphasis on the word picture as on the word big. Historians have recently been drawn as much as economists have been to the distinction between macro and micro, but not all historians and only a few economists think pictorially, as I do, when they draw the distinction. I have also noticed recently that the words 'the bigger picture' are used as frequently as 'the big picture'. I am not sure what the bigger picture really is.

Eventually I decided to call this chapter 'Pasts, Present, Futures'. To me these constitute a threesome. In Dickens's *A Christmas Carol* Marley tells Scrooge to expect visits from three spirits, the ghost of Christ past, the ghost of Christmas present and finally the ghost of Christmas yet to come, to which Scrooge says 'Spirit I fear you most of all.'

As historians we are concerned with all three spirits. There is no agreed version. When we deal with futures we confront alternative possibilities. We can think of them in terms of predictions but more modestly the most we can do is to produce alternative forecasts. The difference between dealing with pasts and futures is that in the past there are events and in the future there are none. More recently we have begun to look at the present in a rather different way, treating it as interesting in itself. It is not merely that it consists of news headlines or of radio programmes like *Today*. Emily Dickinson wrote a poem which includes the lines 'When that which is and that which was / Apart intrinsic stand'.

Past and Present was the title of a remarkable book by the remarkable Scotsman Thomas Carlyle, born in Ecclefechan, Dumfriesshire, in 1795, who has intruded more than once into this book. He was not particularly interested in the future. He wrote *Past and Present* in only seven weeks, probably as a diversion from his massive *Oliver Cromwell*, published in the same year, 1843. Four years earlier he had published his essay on Chartism, to which *Past and Present* was a sequel. It drew on the twelfth-century chronicles of the Abbot of St Edmund's Bury and compared the Abbot's reverence for work and the dignity of labour with the words and deeds of nineteenth-century 'bosses' who exploited their mill workers, treating them merely as 'hands'. The conditions of their monotonous work were enforced by rules, but the discipline of the factory was very different indeed from the discipline of a monastery.

Carlyle believed in heroes and urged the countrymen of his time to become heroic themselves 'in order to esteem heroes rather than quacks'. The first lecture he gave to raise funds for the London Library was 'The Hero as God'. In it he named as his hero the Norse god Odin. He referred also to the ash tree Igdrasil. This was the Tree of Existence, the past, the present and the future, what was doing, what is doing and what will be done, 'the infinite conjunction of the verb *to do*'.

It was not only Carlyle but other early Victorians who made much of the contrast between past and present, often leaving out the future altogether. The Roman Catholic architect Augustus Welby Pugin, born in 1812, drew pictures in 1826 of medieval townscapes with church steeples rising into the heavens and nineteenth-century industrial townscapes with mill chimneys pouring out smoke into polluted skies. Pugin was employed by Sir Charles Barry, architect of the new Houses of Parliament built between 1840 and 1860. Pugin is the subject of an outstanding recent biography by Rosemary Hill.

The last chapter of Carlyle's *Past and Present* was called 'Horoscope', a word that figures in most of today's popular newspapers. Astrology thrives as much as astronomy in what we sometimes call a 'post-industrial' society. Meanwhile, one of the most lively and interesting journals of historical studies to traverse the centuries is named *Past and Present*. In origin a Marxist journal, both Marxists and non-Marxists were represented on its Board from the start. Christopher Hill, Marxist Master of Balliol College, Oxford, was President of the Past and Present Society that founded it.

The number of the journal which I have in front of me, picked out at random, Number 76, August 1977, includes articles on various centuries and brings together different themes and different disciplines. The first article deals with 'Power and society in the lordship of Ireland, 1272–1377', a period just after the chronicles of the Abbot of St Edmund's Bury were completed. (It is amazing that Bury St Edmund has featured in this book, in a quite different context.) The last article in this number of *Past and Present* is by W. D. Rubinstein, writing from the National University of Australia, where I had been Visiting Professor in 1961; it deals with the 'Wealth elites and class structure of modern Britain'.

The article which interests me most is 'Thomas Spence, the Trumpet of Jubilee'. It is by good fortune that I am re-reading it in what is still regarded (just) as the jubilee year of the University of Sussex. I knew of Spence's radical origins in Newcastle and of his book *The Real Reading-Made-Easy* (Newcastle, 1782) which, alas, I have never read. I knew too of his move south from Newcastle to London, where he ran a bookshop, gathered a group of Spenceans, stood trial in 1801, was deemed by the judge to be a seditious eccentric, 'not worthy of hanging', but to successive British wartime governments he and the Spenceans seemed the core of revolutionary conspiracy in London.

He was to figure in Edward Thompson's *Making of the English Working Class*, a book much read by Sussex undergraduates, not all of them radicals and fewer still of them Marxists. For a time Sussex radicals were much in the news. Edward had been a colleague of mine when I was Professor of History at Leeds. He was working then in its Department of Extra-Mural Studies and I managed to get the Director of Extra-Mural Studies, the formidable Professor Raybould, to allow Edward to lecture to my students of history. He never found it easy to keep to timetables, and it was when I was about to board a train from Leeds to St Pancras that he rushed up to me bearing an article for *Essays in Labour History* which I was then co-editing with John Saville, a communist of different convictions from Edward.

I had learnt by then that no two communists are alike. It was as a non-communist President that I formed and held together the Labour History Society, founded in commemoration of G. D. H. Cole, a socialist who was never in any way a communist. Working in the Society I knew before I became President that no two communists were more different than Edward Thompson and Eric Hobsbawm. John Savile was different from both of them, but stayed loyal to the Communist party, as Eric Hobsbawm did, even after the Hungarian uprising of 1956.

The article on Spence in the number of *Past and Present* that I picked up at random, was written by T. R. Knox, and bore the address 'from Bowling Green State University, Ohio'. I associated Bowling Green with pioneering American studies of popular culture, which were being carried out before Birmingham developed its own Centre of Popular Culture. Sadly I have never visited Bowling Green. One of the professors there with whom I frequently corresponded and whose approach to popular culture was very different from mine, shared my unusual first name. He was called Asa Berger. Asa is a threesome name, which I should have mentioned in my first chapter. The tax authorities never believed in it, and they always inserted full stops – A. S. A. I shared the threesome also with the American Security Agency, the Amateur Swimming Association and the Advertising Standards Authority, which has figured at several points in this book.

I have explained in Chapter 5, where I chose retailing as the first of my 'Abiding Historical Interests', how important the study of advertising is in business history and in the history of shops in particular. Naturally when I examined No. 76 of *Past and Present* I turned first to publishers' advertisements with almost as much eagerness as I turned to the articles. The House of Longman, whose history I was to write, covering the whole period from 1724, when it came into existence, to the 1990s, had many advertisements in that number of *Past and Present*. Among them was one for the second edition of a book by a friend of mine Alan Rogers, *Approaches to Local History*, the first edition of which had been written to accompany a BBC radio series given the title *This Was Their World*. In 1974 I had also edited a volume of essays on publishing to celebrate the 250th anniversary of the founding of Longman.

All things connect. Institutional longevity is as interesting to me as individual longevity and far less studied. My own unexpected longevity has enabled me to write *Loose Ends and Extras*, and it is with my own longevity that I will end it. I have not yet finished, however, with *Past and Present* as a title. It is the name given in Sussex to the newsletter, or so it started, of the Sussex Archaeological Society, of which I was briefly president while I was Vice-Chancellor of Sussex University. It is now a beautiful well-illustrated magazine published in Lewes.

As I am concluding the last chapter of *Loose Ends and Extras*, I turn to a number of the Archaeological Society's *Past and Present*, from December 2013. It deals with two interesting aspects of the county's archaeological record. The first is a section on community archaeological 'finds of the year' in 2013, including schoolchildren's finds in a pasture field, Little Stanmer, on the border between the parishes of Newick and Barcombe.

The second has a far longer record. There had been published in 2013 the 150th volume of *Sussex Archaeological Collections*, the brainchild of an early meeting of the Society in 1847. This came into existence in 1847 after the coming of the railway from Lewes to Brighton provided the opportunity for digging up a lot of historically interesting land. The *Collections* have subsequently been edited by twenty-three editors. The most famous of them, L. B. Saltzman, served for fifty years. Sussex, east and west, with Lewes Castle, Michelham

Priory, Anne of Cleves House, Fishbourne Roman Palace and Arundel Castle, is a national and international treasure house.

I have been increasingly interested in my own lifetime in futures. I became involved in futures mainly through five writers, Daniel Bell, I. F. Clarke, Umberto Eco, Isaac Asimov and Kurt Vonnegut. There are many articles and books about all five of them and Vonnegut's letters constitute the autobiography that he never wrote. Daniel Bell was a Professor of Sociology at Harvard, and I have met him many times on both sides of the Atlantic. In the 1960s he became involved in a large-scale American project, that of trying to forecast what would happen at the end of the century and at the beginning of a new millennium. Consciousness of a coming new millennium had as great impact on sociology as on history. Clarke was a most interesting person with whom I corresponded. He wrote most about a future war. Eco was not a sociologist but a semiotician, novelist and literary critic. He is perhaps best known still for his novel *The Name of the Rose* (*Il Nome della Rosa*, 1980), an intellectual mystery combining semiotics, biblical analysis, medieval studies and literary theory. He has been described as 'the Pavarotti of semiotics'. In a later novel, *Foucault's Pendulum* (1988), three under-employed editors working for a minor publishing house develop a conspiracy theory that they call 'the Plan'. A secret order descended from the Knights Templar plot to take over the world.

Isaac Asimov was the first of a group of writers to be published by the remarkable publisher Hugo Gernsback, who went to New York from Luxembourg in 1904, when he was nineteen. In *Modern Electrics* and other magazines he published stories of the kind he called 'scientific fiction'. There is a most interesting study of the science fiction 'family' of the 1930s by Damon Knight called *The Futurians*, published in 1977. Many books have been written about Kurt Vonnegut, and their authors have formulated quite different assessments of his work. He was born in Indianapolis, which made me go to visit that extraordinary city as well as read all his novels. The other place that he put on the map besides Indianapolis was Dresden where he was a prisoner of war and incarcerated in a slaughterhouse.

My interest in science fiction goes back a long way. While I was at Sussex University I took the chair at a conference of science-fiction novelists and was very much impressed by J. G. Ballard, who lived in Shanghai as a boy and has described his experiences there in war and occupation. I noted that science fiction did not start with the futurians I have mentioned. In 1931 H. G. Wells, who had written *The Time Machine* in 1895, wrote a piece called 'Fifty Years Ago' in which he predicted the shape of things to come fifty years hence. It was a gloomy book. 'Gladly would the prophet prophesy pleasant things, but his duty is to tell the world what he sees. He sees a world still firmly controlled by soldiers.'

Truth is certainly stranger than science fiction. David Lodge has transformed the life of Wells into a novel of tangled emotion, which he calls *A Man of Parts*. It is interesting, given the contrasting backgrounds of Lodge and Wells, to speculate about fiction, forecasts, predictions and prophecies. I have been a regular reader of *Futures*, a magazine published in the United States where there is an Institute for the Future. It was first published in 1968, a landmark year in twentieth-century history. I wrote an article for *Futures* in 1977 in which I was more optimistic than Wells. It was called 'From Prophesy to Prediction'.

I went back to the year 1880 when the development of 'seeing by telegraph' or 'by electricity' was predicted. The word 'television' was apparently used for the first time in French in 1900; its first use in English may have been in 1909 when Gernsback used it in *Modern Electrics*. Albert Robida, who wrote much of interest about futures, foresaw public uses – as distinct from private uses – of pictures on the wall; and a writer in *Lightning*, one of the many popular science magazines of the 1890s, explained,

> the grandsons of the present generation will see one another across the Atlantic and the great ceremonial events of the world as they pass before the eyes of the camera, to be executed at the same instant before mankind.

I go on in my article to talk of Baird and of Nikola Tesla, a prophet of the electric age.

In this age nature has become more a matter for futures speculation than it ever had been before I ended *Special Relationships: People and Places* with trees, real trees like the great cedar tree at Tyninghame, and allegorical and metaphysical trees, including trees of life, which were much in my mind before I started the book. I end this book with birds. In my press cuttings on gardening, I read of the importance of treating birds well, beginning with making a garden into a bird haven. Almost every day we hear David Attenborough introducing the tweet of a bird at the end of the *Today* programme.

Many wildlife programmes – and there are now enormous numbers of them – are devoted to the migration of birds, birds coming and going, covering vast distances each way. Why do they do it? How do they do it? What triggers the time when they move? The numbers of birds in our garden are changing. Where are the house sparrows that were once seen in large numbers? What of the starlings, which have been described as Stalin's starlings? What happens to swifts and swallows as they depart in full flight and in large numbers for warmer climes while hefty Hooper swans are arriving in Britain in large numbers from the north?

One of the three men who founded Mass Observation in 1937, Tom Harrisson, started life as an ornithologist before he turned to observing people. Harrisson's two co-founders, thus constituting a threesome, were Charles Madge and Humphrey Jennings. There was a coincidence too at the beginning of this story. Charles Madge wrote a letter to the *New Statesman* urging the need for inviting a group of correspondents in different parts of the country to say what they were doing day by day. Next to Madge's letter was printed a poem by Tom Harrisson, who only published one poem in his life. Harrisson was in Bolton, carrying out field work on industrial life

The Mass Observation Archive is now in the University of Sussex thanks to my own friendship with Harrisson. As Vice-Chancellor I invited him to share the small building where I kept my books and university papers. I provided one room for him to sleep in until he found a house outside. I got to know him very well and we had some good times together. I was in despair when he was killed with his Belgian wife on the way from the Thai outback to Bangkok airport. Since Tom had no relatives I had to make all the necessary arrangements for handling his affairs after death.

There has been much poetry about birds and I have in front of me a recent book, *The Poetry of Birds* (2009), edited by Simon Armitage and Tim Dee. It starts with the ostrich and ends with the phoenix. It includes herons, which I have loved watching in flight in China. Sometimes flying with them are birds not include in Armitage and Dee's anthology, cranes, and cranes in China are symbols of longevity. Liu Zhengcai's paperback, *The History of Longevity*, published by the Foreign Languages Press in Beijing, starts with the sentence 'Chinese people have always cherished life, going for a long life span and accumulated experience in longevity since early antiquity.' The last of his chapters 'On Food Therapy for Longevity' includes chrysanthemums which I drew attention to when I was writing on Fred Goody, who in his book *The Culture of Flowers* (1993) explained that in China chrysanthemums carry a message of long life.

Next year, 2015, will be a landmark year in my own private life, for Susan and I will be celebrating our sixtieth wedding anniversary. What flowers could I give to her?

Appendix 1

In Place of Footnotes

I have written many books without footnotes, *Loose Ends and Extras* being the last of them. Yet I confess that I love footnotes. They figure at the end of each page in *A History of Broadcasting in the United Kingdom*. They were there in *Patterns of Peacemaking* and in the second volume of *The History of Birmingham*. They were as full as I could make them in *The Age of Improvement* (1959 and 2000). Mine are not only footnotes for reference, consisting of the titles of sources I use in my text, but a means of bringing in disputed points of view, persisting but developing arguments and changing perspectives.

My favourite footnotes are the most famous of all footnotes, those of Edward Gibbon in his *Decline and Fall of the Roman Empire*, conceived of in Rome and ended there, a climax described by Gibbon in a magnificent passage of prose in 1785. Gibbon appended no fewer than 7,920 footnotes to his text, a quarter of its length, and to all of them he devoted great attention. Some of them could be judged naughty by his readers. He based his footnote on the Byzantine empress Theodora, wife of the Emperor Justinian, for example, on her origins as a circus girl and a dancer as described in the *Secret History* of Procopius, which was spitefully coloured. Gibbon's massive *Decline and Fall* covers the history of Byzantium as well as the history of Rome and what he wrote of Byzantium is prejudiced and unreliable. Particularly when he focuses on Rome, however, his great book has been much revered by historians of different generations.

In recent years there has been as much talk of the decline and fall of footnotes as of the decline and fall of empires. They are said to put off authors, publishers and readers alike. They began to put me off when Oxford University Press urged me, by then a decade retired from the University, to include footnotes in the published version of my Ford Lectures. These had been delivered in 1991 but I did not immediately offer them to the Press for publication. They were treated as a brand-new book in 2000, and although I duly appended footnotes at their request, the new book never appeared.

I now associate footnotes with press cuttings as well as with books and articles. I was long sent them by an admirable press agency, but now I still keep them regularly day-by-day. In the first days of the University of Sussex my wife kept the press cuttings concerning the University in two impressive albums which she has now handed over to the Vice-Chancellor.

Even given the presence of footnotes a divided bibliography with different categorised sections is useful. I have arranged this in *A History of Broadcasting in the United Kingdom*. In Volume III, for example, *The War of Words*, which I precede with a bibliographic note, I begin with pamphlets and BBC *Year Books*, which continued to be published throughout the war, and add an article by Sir Harold Bishop, 'The War-time Activities of the Engineering Division of the BBC' from the *Journal of the Institution of Electrical Engineers* (1947). Intelligence Papers and Reports, Monitoring Digests and special papers written by Monitors, I go on, 'are new to this volume'. Unfortunately much primary material had been destroyed during the war, particularly material concerning the BBC's Overseas Service.

This is a very sophisticated bibliographical note and, in particular, the section on intelligence and propaganda interests me profoundly. I had to prepare it at a time, 1970, when I was tied by the Official Secrets Act and could say or write nothing about Bletchley Park. I added the briefest of notes to my Postscript of 1994 when a second edition of *The War of Words* was published. I had only just got to know at the time how much the BBC had itself been prevented from broadcasting certain programmes by the authorities and how there were secret agents inside Broadcasting House.

I cannot now leave myself out of the statement on intelligence and propaganda in my long bibliographical note. I served in the Intelligence Corps with Derrick Sington, co-author of *The Goebbels Experiment* (1942). I discussed 'black broadcasting' not only with Dick Crossman (as I still think of R. H.), but with Sefton Delmer. I was a friend of M. R. D. Foot, who wrote *SOE in France* (1966) and much else, and I was an examiner of J. Bennet, whose *British Broadcasting and the Danish Resistance Movement* was also published in 1966. I quoted in my bibliographical note Ivor Thomas's *Warfare by Words*. Ivor was my local MP during the war, and through him I learned more about propaganda than from any propaganda agency. After the war I met French colleagues concerned with propaganda who treated me as a British expert on propaganda. There was no better country than France to study propaganda and to talk and write about it. You soon move out of books altogether into living history.

Appendix 2

By Way of Books

I begin this note with a list of my own books. I regret that I did not do so in *Special Relationships: People and Places*. I am often asked how many books I have written, and have had to answer that I don't know. Now I do. I have mentioned several of my own books in the chapters of *Loose Ends and Extras*. For completeness I incorporate them in this list. Some I co-authored, some co-edited. The latter raise tricky problems with contributors. Some of my own books have gone through more than one edition. Some have been translated into other languages.

1945   *Patterns of Peacemaking*, co-authored with David Thomson and Ernest Meyer.

1952   *The History of Birmingham, 1863–1938*. This was the second volume of a history of the city commissioned by the Birmingham City Council to commemorate the centenary of the incorporation of the borough in 1838, Conrad Gill wrote the first. Although we knew and liked each other, neither of us saw the text of the other's volume before publication.

1954   *Victorian People*.

1956   *Friends of the People*.

1959   *The Age of Improvement*. A fully revised edition appeared in 2000, a unique case of such thorough updating.

1960   *Chartist Studies*. This was the first volume of *Essays in Labour*

History which I co-edited with John Saville. The second and third volumes appeared in 1971 and 1973.

1961 *The Birth of Broadcasting.* This was the first volume of my *History of Broadcasting in the United Kingdom.*
They Saw It Happen, 1897–1940.
A Study of the Life and Work of Seebohm Rowntree.

1963 *Victorian Cities.*

1965 *The Golden Age of Wireless*, the second volume in my *History of Broadcasting in the United Kingdom.*

1967 *William Cobbett.*

1970 *The War of Words, 1939–45*, the third volume in my *History of Broadcasting in the United Kingdom.*
The Nineteenth Century edited by me as part of a Thames and Hudson series on centuries.

1973 *Cap and Bell*, extracts from *Punch*, co-edited with my wife, Susan.

1974 *Essays on the History of Publishing*, a volume edited by me to commemorate the 250th anniversary of the House of Longman.

1979 *Governing the BBC.*
Sound and Vision, 1945–55, the fourth volume of my *History of Broadcasting in the United Kingdom.*
Iron Bridge to Crystal Palace: Impact and Images of the Industrial Revolution.

1982 *The Power of Steam.*
Marx in London.

1983 *A Social History of England.* A third edition, fully revised, appeared in 1999.

1984 *Toynbee Hall: The First Hundred Years.*
Marks & Spencer, 1884–1984.

1985 *Collected Essays*, two volumes:
Vol. 1 *Words, Numbers, Places, People.*
Vol. 2 *Images, Problems, Standpoints, Forecasts.*
Vol. 3, *Serious Pursuits, Communications and Education,*
appeared in 1991.

Wine for Sale: Victoria Wine and the Liquor Trade,
1860–1986.
The BBC: The First Fifty Years.

1986 *The Franchise Affair*, co-authored with Joanna Spicer.

1988 *Victorian Things.*

1989 *A Victorian Portrait: Victorian Life and Values as Seen*
through the Work of Studio Photographs.

1994 *Haut Brion.*

1995 *The Channel Islands, Occupation and Liberation.*
Competition, 1955–74, the fifth and last volume in my *History*
of Broadcasting in the United Kingdom.
Fins de Siècle, How Centuries End, co-edited with Daniel
Snowman.

1997 *Modern Europe, 1789-1989,* co-authored with Patricia Clavin.
A revised and extended edition, *Modern Europe, 1789–2003,*
was published in 2003.

1998 *Chartism.*

2000 *Go to It, Working for Victory on the Home Front.*

2001 *Michael Young, Social Entrepreneur.* Second edition 2005.

2002 *A Social History of the Media from Gutenberg to the Internet,*
co-authored with Peter Burke.

2005 *A History of the Royal College of Physicians of London,*
1945–1983. This was the fourth volume of a history of the
College written and published for the College by different
authors at different times. My volume was totally
independent of the others.

2008 *A History of Longman and Their Books.*

2011 *Secret Days: Code-Breaking in Bletchley Park.*

2012 *Special Relationships: People and Places.*

2014 *Loose Ends and Extras.*

In 1990 a former graduate student of mine, Derek Fraser, edited a
book of essays, *Cities, Class and Communication*, for my forthcoming
seventieth birthday. Derek had been formerly Professor of Modern
History at the University of Bradford and went on to become

Professor of English History at the University of California, Los Angeles. He was – and is – through many subsequent changes in his life, a good friend. *Cities, Class and Communication* included not only a list of my then-published works, but also a list of my contributions to other books, and my introductions and forewords to other books. I wish that I had been able in *Loose Ends and Extras* to bring it up to date. It would have been a valuable extra.

I divide books other than my own into two basic categories – those which I read while I am writing my own books and those which I read quite independently of what I am writing. In both cases I am looking for more than mere information. Having called this book *Loose Ends and Extras* I must start this note with Ned Sherrin. I pick out among his books *A Small Thing – Like an Earthquake* (1983), *Ned Sherrin in His Anecdotage: A Classic Collection from the Master Raconteur* (1993) and, useful as well as interesting, *Ned Sherrin, The Autobiography* (2005). When Ned sadly died of cancer of the throat at the age of seventy-six in 2007 I supplemented his book with obituaries, some broadcast on BBC Radio 4, some appearing in newspapers, including *The Times*, the *Daily Telegraph*, *The Independent*, the *Guardian* and the *New York Times*. I did not write any obituary myself having been struck down in 2002 with deep-vein thrombosis.

I have no space or time in this note to give a long list of books, either of those that have influenced me in my own writings or that I have read independently. I have written two examples of 'The List' of six books at widely separated times for *The Week*. This indispensable publication always includes separately a Book of the Week and under Health & Science an article called 'What the sciences are saying . . .' This has been relevant to me in writing Chapter 3 of this book on the sciences in Sussex University. Such regular title headings are useful. Books that I singled out in my first 'List' included Reinhold Niebuhr's *Moral Man and Immoral Society*, which he had published in 1932 and which influenced me greatly when I was an undergraduate, and Oswald Spengler's *The Decline of the West* (1918) which I was reading the night before I joined the Army. Spengler's theory was that every culture – and he delineated what he considered those cultures to be – passes through a life cycle not different from that of human beings. I would now add to my 'List' David Kahn's *The Codebreakers: The Story of Secret Writing* (1996, revised edition) and W. E. Houghton, *The Victorian Frame of Mind* (1957), which sets out in separate chapters Victorian ideas and attitudes, often conflicting ones.

Novelists have always figured in my reading, as they did in Houghton's. Some I have mentioned in *Loose Ends and Extras*. In this note I draw my readers' attention to Ian McEwan's novels. His *Sweet Tooth* (2012) takes us straight back to Sussex University when he was a student and I was Vice-Chancellor. A near contemporary of his, born in 1946, was a novelist whom I greatly admire, Julian Barnes. I was immediately captivated by his *Metroland* in 1980 and four years later by his *Flaubert's Parrot*. His *The Sense of an Ending* (2011) came out while I was writing *Special Relationships: People and Places*.

I go back further in time to the novelist John Fowles, with whom I had a special relationship, which I described in my *Special Relationships*. Five years younger than me, he was educated at Bedford School which I got to know and in which I felt at home when I was living in Bedford before and after going to Bletchley Park. Fowles's agents, Anthony Shiel Associates, had the acronym ASA. I liked the title of his first published book *The Collector* (1963), a name that could have been given to me. His *The French Lieutenant's Woman* (1969) discerningly and sensitively treated time, and was turned into a striking film, as many of Ian McEwan's books were to be.

The 'hero' of Fowles's last novel (1977), called *Daniel Martin*, bore the Christian name of my elder son. The philosopher in the novel had been teaching at Worcester College Oxford, and he and his wife had lived in a house in Beaumont Street just above the College. Not only does a cottage in Wytham Woods, a great escape from Oxford, to which I had a special pass, figure in the novel, but so too does a flat in Notting Hill Gate in London where Susan and I had acquired a small house.

Long before I had met John Fowles, Susan and I became friends with Penelope Lively. I have read all her many novels, I believe, although in 1954 I had no idea that she would write any. She is now a Statesman of Literature, and I quoted in *Special Relationships: People and Places* her engrossing and disturbing novel *How It All Began* (2011) which I set alongside Julian Barnes's *The Sense of an Ending*.

In her novel, Penelope at her best was contemplating among many other things the old age of her historian non-hero Henry. He had been a fluent lecturer who never used notes. Now he forgets all that he had known of an age, the eighteenth century, on which he has been an authority, 'the last gasp of Namier'. He is humiliated when he tries to give a lecture in Namier's old university, Manchester, and forgets everything about chronology and the names of the century's main historical characters. 'Old age is an insult', he tells his companion, Marion, on the way back to London. 'Old age is a slap in the face.'

I am fascinated by this novel because it deals with an old age quite different from mine, a subject which Penelope has written about in her latest novel *Ammonites and Leaping Fish: A Life in Time* (2013). This ends not with people but with things. I am fascinated too, given my own old age, not only by what she writes about old age in *How It All Began* but by the names that she introduces into that book. A Polish student of English in the novel, Anton, has only been in the country for six weeks working on a building site with no building trades skills. He has read a surprising amount of fiction, including John Updike and Ian McEwan. He likes crime fiction, as I do, and has enjoyed P. D. (Phyllis) James in translation.

I do not need to read my friend Phyllis in translation. She is the last of my friends to be included in 'By Way of Books'. She is several months older than me, and I believe that I have read all her detective novels, beginning with *Cover Her Face* (1962), a year after I arrived in Sussex University. My favourite novel of hers is *Devices and Desires*, published in 1989, a stirring year in world history. From 1988 to 1993 she was an outstanding Governor of the BBC, not afraid to challenge its management and leadership. She has won an immense number of awards as a detective-story writer and many of her novels, like Ian McEwan's, have been filmed.

I end 'By Way of Books' with two non-fiction books on time, which I have used throughout writing *Loose Ends and Extras* – *The History of Time, A Very Short Introduction* (2005) by Leofranc Holford-Strevens and *Mapping Time: The Calendar and its History* (1998) by E. G. Richards.

Index of Names